FAITHFUL
ABUNDANT
TRUE

KAY ARTHUR

PRISCILLA SHIRER

BETH MOORE

With study questions by **Lorie Keene**

LifeWay Press®
Nashville, Tennessee

ISBN 9781415868980
Item 005271629

Dewey Decimal Classification Number: 248.843

Subject Heading: FAITH \ CHRISTIAN LIFE \ SPIRITUAL LIFE

Unless otherwise noted, Scripture quotations used by Kay Arthur are from the New American
Standard Bible: 1995 Update. © The Lockman Foundation, 1960, 1962, 1963, 1968, 1971,
1972, 1973, 1975, 1977, 1995. Used by permission.

Unless otherwise noted, Scripture quotations used by Priscilla Shirer and Beth Moore
are from the Holy Bible, New International Version, copyright © 1973, 1978, 1984
by International Bible Society.

To order additional copies of this resource:
Write LifeWay Church Resources Customer Service; One LifeWay Plaza; Nashville, TN
37234-0113; fax order to (615) 251-5933; call toll free 1-800-458-2772;
e-mail *orderentry@lifeway.com;* order online at *www.lifeway.com;*
or visit the LifeWay Christian Store serving you.

Printed in the United States of America

Leadership and Adult Publishing
LifeWay Church Resources
One LifeWay Plaza
Nashville, Tennessee 37234-0175

Contents

A Word from Your Editor

Welcome to *Faithful, Abundant, True.* When our event team at LifeWay began the Deeper Still events with Kay, Beth, and Priscilla, we all knew God was doing something special. To have these three teachers together is an amazing opportunity indeed, so we began to think about how we could share the chemistry of these three women of God with everyone.

The first result of that collaboration was *Anointed, Transformed, Redeemed*, and we were amazed by the women's response. We immediately began to look forward to the next time we could work with a Deeper Still event.

At the Deeper Still Orlando, we again recorded the teaching sessions along with the fun panel discussion where the three teachers answered questions from attendees. As we listened to the messages at that event, we knew these words needed to be pondered and applied. So once again we set out to create a print and video aid to help women share the experience and get the greatest benefit from the powerful message. However, we immediately faced a daunting challenge: our overloaded authors didn't have time to devote to writing.

We saw the situation as an opportunity to create a special resource that would both share the powerful message from Deeper Still and be short and easily used by busy women. I enlisted the aid of Lorie Keene, a wonderful young author and Bible teacher. Lorie divided the messages into daily segments and wrote learning activities to lead women to unpack and apply the messages. Little did I know that was just the beginning of the story.

Of course you know that Kay, Priscilla, and Beth are among the hardest-working people on the planet. By the time they reviewed our work, all three of them decided to take Lorie's work and make it their own. Kay rewrote the whole two weeks to reflect her distinctive inductive method. Priscilla and Beth both did rewrites to varying degrees. You hold the result. The idea is that you will first listen to the teachers through the medium of video. Then we want to help you unpack the messages through questions and looking to related Scriptures.

Our video team edited the teaching into six sessions plus the panel to use either in a women's retreat where you can recreate your group's own experience of the Orlando Deeper Still event or as a seven-session study.

Just as we've included bonus video features, you'll find some bonus items in this member book. We've included articles from *HomeLife* magazine that will enhance your study or retreat. In the back you'll find plans and suggestions for a retreat and a leader guide for a seven-session study.

Thank you for allowing LifeWay to be your ministry partner. We pray that you will be blessed and changed through this encounter with God's Word.

KAYARTHUR

In the late 1960s a missionary couple in Mexico suffered medical problems and returned home to Chattanooga, Tennessee. Little did they know that God had a greater field of ministry for them. Jack Arthur became station manager for a Christian radio station, and Kay Arthur started a Bible study for teenagers in their living room. By 1970 youth were meeting in a barn they had cleaned out and patched up themselves. Soon adults were coming too.

The first women's Bible study class began, and the word spread. Night classes started. Soon Kay was traveling to Atlanta, Georgia, every week to teach nearly 1,800 adults. Knowing she and Jack would not be able to travel every week, Kay wanted to teach others to study inductively and so began writing Precept Upon Precept courses.

Jack left his radio career and became president and leader of this flourishing new organization. Today Precept Ministries International (*www.precept.org*) reaches into 150 countries with studies in 70 languages for children, teens, and adults.

Through the many ministries of Precept—including the daily radio and television program "Precepts for Life," Kay Arthur had touched millions of lives. A well-known conference speaker and author, Kay has a unique ability to reach people in an exciting, effective way—teaching them how to discover truth for themselves so truth can change their lives and equip them to be used to advance God's kingdom.

ABOUT THE
AUTHORS

PRISCILLASHIRER

Priscilla Shirer is a Bible teacher whose ministry is focused on the expository teaching of the Word of God to women. Her desire is to see women not only know the uncompromising truths of Scripture intellectually but experience them practically by the power of the Holy Spirit. Priscilla is a graduate of the Dallas Theological Seminary with a Master's degree in Biblical Studies. For over a decade she has been a conference speaker for major corporations, organizations, and Christian audiences across the United States and the world.

Priscilla is now in full-time ministry to women. She is the author of *A Jewel in His Crown, A Jewel in His Crown Journal, And We Are Changed: Transforming Encounters with God, He Speaks to Me: Preparing to Hear from God, Discerning the Voice of God: How to Recognize When God Speaks,* and *Can We Talk? Soul-Stirring Conversations with God.* Priscilla is the daughter of pastor, speaker, and well-known author Dr. Tony Evans. She is married to her best friend, Jerry. The couple resides in Dallas with their three young sons, Jackson, Jerry Jr., and Jude. Jerry and Priscilla have founded Going Beyond Ministries, where they are committed to seeing believers receive the most out of their relationships with the Lord.

BETHMOORE

Beth Moore

has written best-selling Bible studies on Esther, David, Moses, Paul, Isaiah, Daniel, John, and Jesus. Her books *Breaking Free, Praying God's Word,* and *When Godly People Do Ungodly Things* have all focused on the battle Satan is waging against Christians. *Believing God, Loving Well,* and *Living Beyond Yourself* have focused on how Christians can live triumphantly in today's world. In *Stepping Up* Beth leads Christians to reach a new level of relationship and intimacy with God. Beth has a passion for Christ, a passion for Bible study, and a passion to see Christians living the lives Christ intended.

Beth is an active member of First Baptist Church of Houston, Texas. The wife of Keith, mother of two young adult daughters Melissa and Amanda, and grandmother of Jackson and Annabeth, Beth serves a worldwide audience through Living Proof Ministry. Her conference ministry, writing, and videos reach millions of people every year.

Lorie Keene

holds a Masters of Divinity and a Masters of Theology (Th.M) from The Southern Baptist Theological Seminary. Lorie served as the assistant director of the Women's Program at Southern for three years, prior to becoming a full-time stay-at-home mom to her new son, Elijah. Lorie currently lives in Tullahoma, Tennessee, where her husband Stephen is on staff at Highland Baptist Church as a student/education pastor.

HomeLife Magazine

The *HomeLife* team is thrilled to partner with LifeWay Women to bring you *Faithful Abundant True*. For 63 years *HomeLife* has featured articles about God's amazing faithfulness, His ability to do abundantly more than we could ever imagine, and the wisdom found in His Word. To enhance your study time with Kay, Priscilla, and Beth, we've included three *HomeLife* articles in *Faithful Abundant True*.

FAITHFUL

"I Will Carry You" (p. 28) shares the story of Audrey Caroline, a baby girl who lived only two hours but, in her mother's words, "probably brought more people to the Lord than I will in my lifetime." Angie continues, "As soon as Audrey was woven in my womb, she was a child. She was my child. And yet, she wasn't. She was God's all along, and I bowed to that fact every day I carried her." Audrey's story is a memorial of the faithfulness of God and an example of the faithfulness demanded in Hebrews.

ABUNDANT

"The Other Side of Darkness" (p. 74) illustrates God's ability to redeem even the darkest moments of our lives. Brigitte Kitenge, a Rwandan genocide survivor, endured unspeakable tortures. Today she says, "When I see the scars on my body, I see the work of the evil one, but I also see grace springing through each of my scars. I bless my torturers and praise God for His deliverance, restoration, and grace."

TRUE

"The Pull of Riptide Friendships" (p. 118) encourages you to ask yourself, "Do I move my friends toward myself or toward Jesus?" Counselor Cheryl Baird explains, "If you've become the focal point and are therefore pulling [your friends] away from God, you need to take a step back." This woman-to-woman article shines biblical light on the need for spiritual and relational discernment in everyday life.

The *HomeLife* team prays these articles invigorate your personal walk with Christ and your ministry to others by reminding you that God is, indeed, *Faithful, Abundant, & True.*

FAITHFUL

KAYARTHUR

SESSION 1

VIEWERGUIDE

1. Jesus keeps everything in this world in place by the power of _____ _____.

2. *Ichabod* means "The _____ has _____."

3. The eternal Word of God is _____ _____ for and _____ for.

4. Are you prepared for the persecution?

5. The people of God were not _____ as Christians and

were actually _____.

GROUP DISCUSSION QUESTIONS

1. What are some of the characteristics, qualities, and authority that we attribute
   to God and to Jesus Christ as well?

2. What most helps you keep on track maturing in your faith?

WEEK ONE | DAY ONE
Are We Listening?

God, seated on His throne (Heb. 1:3) is *El Olam* (Gen. 21:33)—the everlasting God. He has no beginning, and He knows no end. He is the Alpha and the Omega. He lives and rules forever in righteousness. He is *Elohim,* your Creator.

El Olam is making intercession for you. If you want to go deeper still, then we must pay close attention to what He has said, fixing our eyes on Jesus, the author and perfecter of our faith. After listening to the teaching the Father gave me for you, do you realize how God treasures you? You are so precious that God would speak to you through His Son. In these next two weeks of study I pray you will allow me to take you deeper into the Word of God. It is my passion that …

- you truly hear in the depths of your heart and mind the word of God
- you discover *for yourself* what God has spoken
- discovering this truth for yourself, you will desire with all your heart, soul, mind, body, and spirit to live accordingly, to live in the "rest of faith"

Although your assignments for each day are not lengthy, they are designed to impact your life in a lasting way. The benefit and blessing you receive will be according to your commitment, your disciplined faithfulness, and perseverance. Even as I write, I am seeking the Father on your behalf.

As I prayed about my message for Deeper Still, God made it clear that I was to read to the audience the entire first chapter of Hebrews. This, beloved, is where we will begin. I want you to observe Hebrews 1 for yourself. However, before we begin, you need to understand exactly what you are reading. The words written in Hebrews 1, like all the Bible, are the very words God breathed through the unknown person who was His scribe for the Book of Hebrews.

I believe we would be more diligent about studying the Bible—about paying closer attention to Jesus as Hebrews 1:1-2; 2:1-3 says—if we realized that the Bible is God's Word—not man's.

Therefore, let's explore several Scriptures that will help us value even more what we will see tomorrow in Hebrews 1. For the sake of continuity, since people use so many different translations of the Bible, please read the Scriptures listed below from the New American Standard Version.

> Underline or put a box around every reference to the Word of God, including pronouns and synonyms (such as Scripture). You could use a symbol like this ⌒⌒ . Or pick a color and color it the same in all the texts. I am into colors as they are good for identification and recall. Then, in bullet points, under summary list

what you learned from the text about the Word of God. Nothing
more, nothing less. Just the facts. Here we go.

You have had to deal with doubts. Among other things, Satan is a tempter and a liar. He not only tempts and lies to you, he also tempted Jesus. If we can see how Jesus handled the Devil, we can do the same. Therefore, our first Scripture will be Matthew 4:2-4. The part in capital letters is a quote from Deuteronomy 8:3.

Matthew 4:2-4

²And after He had fasted forty days and forty nights, He then became hungry.
³And the tempter came and said to Him, "If You are the Son of God, command that these stones become bread."
⁴But He answered and said, "It is written, 'MAN SHALL NOT LIVE ON BREAD ALONE, BUT ON EVERY WORD THAT PROCEEDS OUT OF THE MOUTH OF GOD.'"

By the way, when you marked "word," did you notice where that word came from? Write it down.

SUMMARY:

2 Timothy 3:16-17

¹⁶All Scripture is inspired by God and profitable for teaching, for reproof, for correction, for training in righteousness;
¹⁷so that the man of God may be adequate, equipped for every good work.

SUMMARY:

2 Peter 1:20-21

²⁰But know this first of all, that no prophecy of Scripture is a matter of one's own interpretation,
²¹for no prophecy was ever made by an act of human will, but men moved by the Holy Spirit spoke from God.

SUMMARY:

John 17:14-17 is what Jesus prayed to His Father before He went to the garden of Gethsemane where He would be betrayed by Judas, arrested, and crucified the next day. Watch the Evil One (Satan, the Devil) in this passage. I mark him with a red pitchfork! By the way, "they" includes you and me (John 17:20). *Sanctify* means to set apart, to consecrate for God—it's another word for *holy!*

John 17:14-17

[14]"I have given them Your word; and the world has hated them, because they are not of the world, even as I am not of the world.

[15]"I do not ask You to take them out of the world, but to keep them from the evil one.

[16]"They are not of the world, even as I am not of the world.

[17]"Sanctify them in the truth; Your word is truth."

SUMMARY:

Hebrews 4:12

[12]For the word of God is living and active and sharper than any two-edged sword, and piercing as far as the division of soul and spirit, of both joints and marrow, and able to judge the thoughts and intentions of the heart.

SUMMARY:

1 Thessalonians 2:13

[13]For this reason we also constantly thank God that when you received the word of God which you heard from us, you accepted it not as the word of men, but for what it really is, the word of God, which also performs its work in you who believe.

Did you mark the "its" the same way you marked the Word? If not, go back and get them.

SUMMARY:

Now then, beloved. Now that you have diligently observed the text and discovered what it said for yourself, think about what you learned about the Word of God, the Bible! Review what you've seen; think about it.

If the Bible is what it says it is—and comes straight from the mouth of God—how important is it that you pay close attention to it? Have you? Have you honored it as it should be honored? Or have you preferred the writings—the books of men and women—above God's Word?

So Great a Salvation

Through the ages people waited for the coming of the Promised One, the Messiah who would bruise the head of the serpent (Gen. 3:1-15). Then in the fullness of time God spoke to us through His Son (Gal. 4:4). Surely we must pay close attention to what He said. What awesome truth you are about to explore as you observe Hebrews 1! Hebrews was written for those who believe in Jesus Christ, those who live this side of the cross. It was written for you, beloved of God.

Part of God's book, Hebrews' purpose is to transform you into the likeness of Jesus, the beloved Son of God, and to equip you to handle every and any situation of life—including the most difficult of circumstances. It is going to teach you what Scripture calls *the rest of faith*.

Today you not only have the privilege of reading through and observing the main characters of Hebrews 1:1–2:3, but you also have the promise that His Spirit will lead and guide you into all truth (John 16:13). Begin today's study in prayer, telling God what is on your heart and what you need to know to understand.

> Read the following text and color every reference to God (the Father) yellow or the color you choose. If you don't have colors, then use a triangle, but color is easier to identify. Make sure you mark all pronouns and synonyms in the same way (for example, Majesty on high is a synonym for God). As you mark the pronouns, make sure it is a reference to God the Father and not God the Son. It can be a little confusing so if you don't know, don't mark it until you do.

> Put a cross † (in red if you can) over every reference to the Son. Don't miss any pronouns or synonyms (such as Lord and God).

Dear One, as you read, remember this is the bread by which you live. Feast!

Hebrews 1:1–2:3

¹God, after He spoke long ago to the fathers in the prophets in many portions and in many ways,

²in these last days has spoken to us in His Son, whom He appointed heir of all things, through whom also He made the world.

³And He is the radiance of His glory and the exact representation of His nature, and upholds all things by the word of His power. When He had made purification of sins, He sat down at the right hand of the Majesty on high,

⁴having become as much better than the angels, as He has inherited a more excellent name than they.

⁵For to which of the angels did He ever say, "You are My Son, today I have begotten You"? And again, "I will be a Father to Him and He shall be a Son to Me"?

⁶And when He again brings the firstborn into the world, He says, "AND LET ALL THE ANGELS OF GOD WORSHIP HIM."

⁷And of the angels He says, "WHO MAKES HIS ANGELS WINDS, AND HIS MINISTERS A FLAME OF FIRE."

⁸But of the Son He says, "YOUR THRONE, O GOD, IS FOREVER AND EVER, AND THE RIGHTEOUS SCEPTER IS THE SCEPTER OF HIS KINGDOM.

⁹"YOU HAVE LOVED RIGHTEOUSNESS AND HATED LAWLESSNESS; THEREFORE GOD, YOUR GOD, HAS ANOINTED YOU WITH THE OIL OF GLADNESS ABOVE YOUR COMPANIONS."

¹⁰AND, "YOU, LORD, IN THE BEGINNING LAID THE FOUNDATION OF THE EARTH, AND THE HEAVENS ARE THE WORKS OF YOUR HANDS;

¹¹THEY WILL PERISH, BUT YOU REMAIN; AND THEY ALL WILL BECOME OLD LIKE A GARMENT,

¹²AND LIKE A MANTLE YOU WILL ROLL THEM UP; LIKE A GARMENT THEY WILL ALSO BE CHANGED. BUT YOU ARE THE SAME, AND YOUR YEARS WILL NOT COME TO AN END."

¹³But to which of the angels has He ever said, "SIT AT MY RIGHT HAND, UNTIL I MAKE YOUR ENEMIES A FOOTSTOOL FOR YOUR FEET"?

¹⁴Are they not all ministering spirits, sent out to render service for the sake of those who will inherit salvation?

²:¹For this reason we must pay much closer attention to what we have heard, so that we do not drift away from it.

²For if the word spoken through angels proved unalterable, and every transgression and disobedience received a just penalty,

³how will we escape if we neglect so great a salvation? After it was at the first spoken through the Lord, it was confirmed to us by those who heard.

We always tell our Precept students that when you observe the Scriptures you always want to focus on the five W's and an H: *who, what, when, where, why,* and *how.* You've already marked two very important who's: God and the Son. But you saw a third who, didn't you? One that Jesus was compared with—angels.

Read through the text again—aloud (it helps you retain what you read). This time mark or color the references to the angels.

Now once you've marked the text, you will want to find out what you learn from marking *God the Father, the Son,* and *the angels.* You do this by looking at your markings and then making a list of what you learn from this portion of God's Word about them.

On the next page list what you learn about God, about the Son, and about angels just from marking the passage. Include nothing more, nothing less. As you make your list, you'll find it helpful to put the verse number beside what you observed from each marking. This way when you review your list, you'll know where your insight came from.

If a truth is listed under The Son but it also relates to God, you need not list it in both columns. Just get it down. Let me give you an example. In verse 3 the emphasis is on the Son; therefore, list the facts under The Son.

Now then, let me get you started! Oh but I would love to do this with you. What a joyous time we would have! I would love to see your eyes and hear you share your insights. And I would love to hug your necks. You and your growth in the knowledge of God is so very precious to me.

GOD THE FATHER	THE SON	ANGELS
v. 1 I spoke to the fathers in the prophets in many portions and many ways	v. 2 was appointed heir of all things v. 2 God made the world through Him	v. 5 Never addressed by God as His begotten Son

Now use what you've found to worship the Father and the Son. In John 4:23 Jesus said we are to worship Him in spirit and truth. Look at the truths you've recorded and remember this is truth. It will never change; God is immutable. He is *El Olam,* the everlasting God. You can always trust Him to be God.

Oh beloved, did you see it? Write it down? "When He [Jesus] had made purification of sins, He sat down at the right hand of the Majesty on high" (Heb. 1:3). Oh the riches of salvation consolidated in these words! Jesus, who knew no sin, was made to be sin for you so that you might be made the righteousness of God (2 Cor. 5:21).

Jesus became man—a human being—that He might bear your sins before His Father as your merciful and faithful high priest and make propitiation for your sins (Heb. 2:17). His sacrifice satisfied the holiness of God. Through Jesus' death for your sins, you were forever freed from Satan's power—the power of death. Why? Because your sins—past, present and future—were paid for in full. Jesus' work of redemption was accomplished in His death, burial, and resurrection; thus He sat down at His Father's right hand, the place of power and authority.

It's the Son who sits there, not angels. He's making intercession for you (Heb. 7:25). Surely you want to pay close attention to Him—to go deeper still.

To Suffer for His Sake

Are you suffering because you are a Christian? Have you, like those in the Book of Hebrews, endured a great conflict of suffering? Has your suffering been because your husband or your kids walked away because they don't like something about you? about your Christianity?

What about your co-workers? friends and acquaintances in general? Are you shunned, talked about, laughed at, despised, rejected, exploited? It's not easy, is it? If you're like me, I've wondered what I've done wrong. How I could have shared or lived my faith more effectively?

As you heard when you listened to the first portion of my message, I understand the rejection, the pain, the loneliness, the angst. My firstborn won't have anything to do with me. He has shut off all communication. My sister tolerates me at a distance, and my brother flat out doesn't want a thing to do with me. He doesn't approve of me—he's sided with my son.

I share that only so you will know you are not alone. We are not the first to suffer and won't be the last. So how do we handle it, live through it, or with it?

The Book of Hebrews, written as an exhortation to those enduring a great conflict of suffering, has the answer. So let's dig deeper still and see what we can learn that will help us endure even as the Son of God endured—and as all true children of God are to endure.

Whenever you study a New Testament letter, you want to learn all you can about the recipients of that letter. To interpret Hebrews correctly, this is imperative. The best way to do that is to read through the epistle, color code every reference to the recipients, and then list all you learned from the text.

Now, don't panic, darling! I am not going to ask you to read through the entire Book of Hebrews and do that. I know that in this study your time is limited. You can go deeper still later if you like. For now I am going to take us, as I did in my message, to Hebrews 10 where we find a good synopsis of the recipients of this letter. In doing so, you and I will gain an understanding of why the author wrote what he wrote and why God has preserved it for His children.

Of course, by now you know why I am taking you to the text of Hebrews; you're smiling, aren't you? You've heard me; you are on to me! I want you, precious one, to discover truth for yourself so that you will know that you know this is what God says. So you are convinced this is what God says so you will not be led astray in these last critical epochal days.

> Pray and begin. Read Hebrews 10:32-39 and color or underline every reference to the people the author was writing to. Mark every "you," "your," and mark the "we" in verse 39 the same color.

Hebrews 10:32-39

[32]But remember the former days, when, after being enlightened, you endured a great conflict of sufferings,

³³partly by being made a public spectacle through reproaches and tribulations, and partly by becoming sharers with those who were so treated.

³⁴For you showed sympathy to the prisoners and accepted joyfully the seizure of your property, knowing that you have for yourselves a better possession and a lasting one.

³⁵Therefore, do not throw away your confidence, which has a great reward.

³⁶For you have need of endurance, so that when you have done the will of God, you may receive what was promised.

³⁷FOR YET IN A VERY LITTLE WHILE, HE WHO IS COMING WILL COME, AND WILL NOT DELAY.

³⁸BUT MY RIGHTEOUS ONE SHALL LIVE BY FAITH; AND IF HE SHRINKS BACK, MY SOUL HAS NO PLEASURE IN HIM.

³⁹But we are not of those who shrink back to destruction, but of those who have faith to the preserving of the soul.

Now read the text again—this time aloud. As you do, see if anything answers the question when, or indicates a sequence of time such as *later, after,* or *then.* Circle it. When I mark my Bible, I mark all references to time with a green circle like this ⏰.

Now, diligent student of His Word, make your list. What do you learn about the recipients, and what are the author's instructions to them? You might put your insights under two different headings:

INFORMATION ABOUT THE RECIPIENTS

INSTRUCTION(S)—EXHORTATION(S) TO THE SAINTS

If we carefully observed Hebrews from chapter 1 up to this point, you could almost surmise their suffering. However, Hebrews 10:32-34 nails the fact that they had suffered. The "after" tells us their suffering was in the past. It was a varied suffering as your list shows you. Everyone did not experience the same thing. Remember that, dear one, we all suffer but it is in various ways. James 1:2-4 calls them "various" trials. In the case of Hebrews some had apparently been put in prison. Hebrews 13:3 supports this with the exhortation to "remember the prisoners, as though in prison with them, and those who are ill-treated" since they are fellow believers.

Have you ever experienced suffering in any of those ways? If so, put a check beside them.

Are there any other ways you have suffered because of being a child of God and living like you truly belong to Jesus?

How did you handle the suffering?

Endurance—not fainting, giving up, shrinking back, drifting away, or walking away—is the will of God. You may be weak, you may be trembling, your knees may be knocking, your voice may be weak and squeaky high with fear, but hang in there. Don't give up. Persevere.

According to the verses you just read, how does God feel about those who shrink back?

What does God have for those who keep their confidence in the Lord and endure?

You can know, if it is the will of God that you endure, then you can do it. Our sovereign God does not permit any temptation you cannot endure. Memorize 1 Corinthians 10:13. Look it up and write it on a card you can take with you.

So how does a "righteous one" live? What does verse 38 tell you?

The Scriptures were written with no chapter or verse divisions in the text; these were added much later. So without a break, what you just observed in Hebrews 10:32-39 would flow right into the faith chapter, Hebrews 11. *Faith* is the key word in this chapter. A key word is an important repeated word in the text that helps you unlock the meaning of the text.

We are going to come back and look at Hebrews 11 later; however, I want you to see what Hebrews 11:6 says about faith before we move on. Read it and put a symbol like this △ over faith.

Hebrews 11:6

⁶And without faith it is impossible to please Him, for he who comes to God must believe that He is and that He is a rewarder of those who seek Him.

Now read it again aloud. This time mark the references to God. Either color them the same color or put a triangle over them. Then list below what you learn from marking God.

Now do you see the importance of faith, beloved? Talk to God about it and then tomorrow I want you to see why God had to say what He was saying to them.

Living by Faith

God tells us in 2 Timothy 3 that difficult times will come, and with that He goes on to describe those times. However, no matter how difficult, you and I are to live by faith. This is why the author of Hebrews quoted Habakkuk 2:4 reminding us that "The righteous will live by his faith." And if we shrink back, God says, "My soul has no pleasure in him."

O beloved, don't you want to bring God pleasure?

Yesterday you saw what the recipients of the letter of Hebrews endured. But what about us? Those who are living even closer to the end of days, what I often refer to as "the last of the last days." When Paul wrote his final letter to his son in the faith, he wanted Timothy to know and to be prepared for what was coming. And what was essential for Paul's disciple Timothy is also essential for us. So let's take a moment and look at 2 Timothy 3. As you read the text below, circle the reference to women.

2 Timothy 3:1-7

[1]But realize this, that in the last days difficult times will come.
[2]For men will be lovers of self, lovers of money, boastful, arrogant, revilers, disobedient to parents, ungrateful, unholy,
[3]unloving, irreconcilable, malicious gossips, without self-control, brutal, haters of good,
[4]treacherous, reckless, conceited, lovers of pleasure rather than lovers of God,
[5]holding to a form of godliness, although they have denied its power; Avoid such men as these.
[6]For among them are those who enter into households and captivate weak women weighed down with sins, led on by various impulses,
[7]always learning and never able to come to the knowledge of the truth.

The character of the world in the last days isn't very pretty, is it? This is what people without God will be like more and more as the end of days approaches. Read through the text again and underline anything that you already see in our culture today.

Did you know that God uses His Word to wash and make us clean? Ephesians 5:26 tells us this. Therefore, read 2 Timothy 3:1-7 one more time and see if there's any place you need cleansing. Examine yourself and make sure you don't see any of these things creeping into your life or into the life of your family. If you do, ask God what you need to do so that it is stopped immediately.

On the next page jot down anything you want to remind yourself about or write out a prayer to our Father about the situation. Spill your heart out to Him and know He will hear.

Since we are women and women are mentioned specifically in this passage, look at where you marked women and list what you learned from the text about them.

They were women led by their impulses rather than truth—the Word of God. What about you? What are you led by? On what do you base your decisions? Have you really gotten on with knowing God or do you want just enough Bible study to get you through your issues? Is Bible study truly changing you?

Do you remember yesterday when we looked at Hebrews 10? Look at verses 10:35-39 in your Bible (or from yesterday's lesson) and read it again aloud.

In Hebrews 10:38, the writer of Hebrews quoted Habakkuk 2:4. It was also quoted by Paul in Romans 1:17 and Galatians 3:11. It was the quote in Romans 1:17 that brought Martin Luther to genuine faith as he sought again to appease God through his works.

Take a minute and look up Habakkuk 2:4 in your Bible and highlight it or mark it in a special way.

Habakkuk questioned God about the difficult times. God replied that it was going to get worse because of the nation of Israel's disobedience. Consequently, God was going to bring the Babylonians against His covenant people. They were breaking His covenant, the law mentioned in Hebrews 2:1-3, and God had to judge them because God's holiness demands judgment. Sin cannot be covered! Remember this: God must judge sin. Believers are not exempt! Judgment begins with the household of God! Grace covers sin, but it doesn't condone it!

So Habakkuk was to write God's message on a tablet all could read (2:1-3). The righteous were to live by faith. They were to believe and to obey God's Word.

Habakkuk's response to the difficult times that were coming is beautiful and worth memorizing so the Spirit of God can bring it to mind when you need it.

Habakkuk 3:16-19

[16]I heard and my inward parts trembled, At the sound my lips quivered. Decay enters my bones, And in my place I tremble. Because I must wait quietly for the day of distress, For the people to arise who will invade us. [17]Though the fig tree should not blossom And there be no fruit on the vines, Though the yield of the olive should fail And the fields produce no food, Though the flock should be cut off from the fold And there be no cattle in the stalls, [18]Yet I will exult in the LORD, I will rejoice in the God of my salvation. [19]The Lord GOD is my strength, And He has made my feet like hinds' feet, And makes me walk on my high places.

When you read Habakkuk's response to the coming difficulties, what do you learn? List the main points of what he said.

That, beloved, is faith's obedience. Things haven't changed. We are to do the same. Remember what you learned about faith in Hebrews 11:6? Review is part of the learning process. Now let's return to Hebrews 10:39.

What do you learn from this verse about those who have faith?

A note in the New American Standard says that *preserving the soul* could also be translated *possessing the soul*. Remember, I talked about this in my message. The phrase *possessing your soul* conveys a distinct idea. The term pictures a person controlling his or her emotions and thoughts.

This means if you cling to God's Word—believe Him, obey Him, not turn away no matter how difficult it gets—you will be able to preserve, to possess your soul. Your soul is what makes you, you. Faith wins! It keeps your heart and mind under control. This is what Habakkuk was doing in his declaration of faith.

With faith, you can remain faithful no matter what you encounter. I just started to write, "Believe me; it's true. God has sustained me through things I never expected to experience." But it would be wrong of me to expect you to take my word when you are to believe God because He is God. The testimonies of others are helpful, encouraging, and we love them, but God and His Word are enough. The problem is we often prefer the stories above His Word.

What happens when you don't persevere in faith? In a difficult situation, if instead of clinging to the Word and walking as God says, you walk your own way, do your own thing, the result will be that you are not possessing your soul.

When you fail to possess your soul, you'll find yourself on a very destructive path! If a person finally turns away and refuses to believe God, then as Hebrews 10:39 says, it leads to destruction—eternal destruction.

However, the writer of Hebrews was convinced that they, like him, were genuine believers—"those who have faith to the preserving of the soul!"

The author of Hebrews had already spoken of the perseverance of genuine faith although he didn't use the word *perseverance*. Read Hebrews 3:6 and 14 below. As you do, put a box around "hold fast," underline "the end," and circle "if."

Hebrews 3:6
⁶But Christ was faithful as a Son over His house—whose house we are, if we hold fast our confidence and the boast of our hope firm until the end.

Hebrews 3:14
¹⁴For we have become partakers of Christ, if we hold fast the beginning of our assurance firm until the end.

What was God saying? What does the text say about those of His house, those who are partakers of Christ?

As we bring today's study to a close, talk to God about your faith.

1 John 5:4-5
⁴For whatever is born of God overcomes the world; and this is the victory that has overcome the world—our faith. ⁵Who is the one who overcomes the world, but he who believes that Jesus is the Son of God?

Pressing on to Maturity

"You have become dull of hearing."

I now know what that means physically and I cannot do a thing about it but get a hearing aid. But God forbid it should describe me spiritually!

The dullness of hearing in Hebrews was the condition of once-enlightened people who had endured a great conflict of suffering for their faith. However, where they once were willing to go to prison for their faith, they were now in danger of drifting away. What about you? Are you in danger of drifting?

If you read Hebrews and color code all the references to the author and to the recipients, you will find very little about the author. We've already dug into Hebrews 10:32-39. You saw the recipients were a people who had suffered and who were being urged to persevere—to live by faith. But why the exhortation?

The answer to that question is critical for us because frankly I believe it is where a great majority are in the United States of America. Consequently people today are ill prepared for the days that are upon us and are yet to come.

Although we explored Hebrews 5:11-14 in the video, I want you to observe the passage yourself so its truths go to the joints and marrow of your being and become a discerner of the thoughts and intents of your heart. Please know, I do it out of love. Love to Him, love for the church of Jesus Christ, and love for you.

As you read Hebrews 5:11–6:2 below, note the "him" in verse 11 is a reference to Melchizedek, who was a priest in the days of Abraham—a priest like Jesus rather than Aaron. (Heb. 5:1-10 gives clearer context for Heb. 5:11-14).

Underline every reference to the recipients. Don't miss the contrast in verses 13-14.

Hebrews 5:11-14

11Concerning him we have much to say, and it is hard to explain, since you have become dull of hearing.

12For though by this time you ought to be teachers, you have need again for someone to teach you the elementary principles of the oracles of God, and you have come to need milk and not solid food.

13For everyone who partakes only of milk is not accustomed to the word of righteousness, for he is an infant.

14But solid food is for the mature, who because of practice have their senses trained to discern good and evil.

Hebrews 6:1-2

1Therefore leaving the elementary teaching about the Christ, let us press on to maturity, not laying again a foundation of repentance from dead works and of faith toward God,

2of instruction about washings and laying on of hands, and the resurrection of the dead and eternal judgment.

Now you know what you need to do next, don't you? List what you learn about the recipients. Making a list helps you not to gloss over the details but to see exactly what God wants you to know.

List what you learned from "the contrast" between the infant and the mature.

The Infant   The Mature

Now summarize the condition of the recipients.

Did you notice what God considers milk in 6:1-2?

As you observed these Scriptures from Hebrews, what was the Spirit of God saying to your heart? Are you going forward or backward in your spiritual growth?

Have people tried to discourage you from in-depth Bible studies saying they are too hard? Or that you just don't have time because you're too busy or you have little ones to care for? What do you think about such statements now? Who, knowing the Word of God, would tell you such things?

O dear heart, remember you are to live on His Word. All of it! He gave us 66 books. How many do you think He wants us to know?

The Bible's truth sustains you, keeps you, sets you apart for a life that pleases Him, a life that is holy, consecrated to God. Knowing God, knowing truth because you have dug it out for yourself, determining to study the Bible book by book will help you be what God has called you to be—a godly woman, a godly wife, a godly mother, a godly example in the church or marketplace.

Someday every Christian will stand at the judgment seat of Christ (Rom. 14:10; 2 Cor. 5:10). If that were to happen today or tomorrow, what would you say to Him in respect to what you've done with His Word?

Now take a few minutes and dig a little deeper into what God's Word says on the subject. Just know that if what follows seems fundamental, foundational to you—it is! Foundations are critical to the stability of a building. Read the following verses from 1 Peter and 1 Corinthians. Pay attention to the references to the recipients as you did in Hebrews.

Put a tall box over milk (or a milk bottle). Underline any reference to solid food.

1 Peter 2:1-2

[1]Therefore, putting aside all malice and all deceit and hypocrisy and envy and all slander,
[2]like newborn babies, long for the pure milk of the word, so that by it you may grow in respect to salvation

What did you learn from marking the words in these verses?

What do you think verse 1 has to do with the subject of growing in salvation?

Are you convicted by the Spirit of God in any way as you read these verses from 1 Peter? If so, how?

1 Corinthians 3:1-4

[1]And I, brethren, could not speak to you as to spiritual men, but as to men of flesh, as to infants in Christ.
[2]I gave you milk to drink, not solid food; for you were not yet able to receive it. Indeed, even now you are not yet able,
[3]for you are still fleshly. For since there is jealousy and strife among you, are you not fleshly, and are you not walking like mere men?
[4]For when one says, "I am of Paul," and another, "I am of Apollos," are you not mere men?

The Corinthian church had some very real problems: immorality, quarrels, divisions, just to name a few. The culture they lived in and were saved out of is very much like ours. I wrote a Precept course on 1 Corinthians because it is a book we so desperately need to study today. The parallels are astounding. How we need the wisdom and instruction in this book!

List what you learn from marking the Corinthians in the verses.

Now drop the plumb line of truth next to your life. How would you rate yourself in comparison with the Corinthians?

Now, precious one, if anyone discourages you from going deeper still into the Word of God, what are you going to do? Who are you going to listen to? Do you know why you will persevere?

I Will ~ Carry You

By
Angie
Smith

photos courtesy of Uchida Photography and Angela C. Smith

> As soon as Audrey was woven in my womb, she was a child. She was my child. And yet, she wasn't. She was God's all along, and I bowed down to that fact every day I carried her.

IT WAS A CRISP JANUARY DAY in 2008 as we headed to our 20-week ultrasound. My husband, Todd, and I had been to several of these. We never got to go to our first because we miscarried, but at the second one we learned that we were having twin girls. A few years later, we found out we were having another girl. With this baby, we had already found out the gender (surprise … it's another girl!) and were just going in to have a more in-depth look at her.

As we settled into our appointment and the technician looked at the screen, we knew something was terribly wrong. Her face was contorted and she asked me a few yes-or-no questions. I finally blurted out, "Is she going to live?"

She mumbled under her breath, but I caught a few bits and pieces.

"I don't know, she's, well, she doesn't, ummm … let me get the doctor, please."

She left and the room spun as I collapsed on Todd's lap.

Shortly after, the doctor confirmed that our sweet baby, Audrey Caroline, was not "compatible with life." Her kidneys were non-functioning, she appeared to be missing several organs, and her heart, which was taking up about 80 percent of her chest, didn't appear to have all four chambers. Because I had no amniotic fluid, her lungs would not develop. The bottom line was that she could not survive outside the womb.

Todd and I were numb with shock, grasping for any words that would make sense in the chaos. The doctor shuffled us in to meet with a genetic counselor, who suggested that we terminate the pregnancy. I use the word *suggested* loosely. They wanted me to check into the hospital that day and have an abortion.

As the doctor explained the situation, and the fact that our baby might be in pain as she grew, Todd and I shook our heads, unable to comprehend the fact that she was kicking inside me as they told us she was going to die. I remember the genetic counselor saying it was hopeless.

I do not serve a God who allows the world to determine what is hopeless.

We scheduled a follow-up visit and met with a wonderful doctor I've known for years. He sadly confirmed the diagnosis and asked us what we wanted to do. There was no question.

Audrey Caroline was ours, and until the Lord told us differently, we would fight for her to live.

Over the next several months, we loved our precious baby the best we could. We talked to her as we watched movies, brought her to the beach and even to Disney World (at our daughter Ellie's request). We made Audrey a part of our lives, and even had a toy bunny we called "Audrey-bunny" to represent her. It had a mark on its heart, and we bandaged it up one night as we prayed for healing.

We believed Audrey could be healed if God so chose, but we needed to prepare for the reality that she might not be. I will never forget walking through a cold cemetery and absent-mindedly pointing to a plot before running to the car and screaming as the doors shut. Audrey was inside me and she was alive, and yet I was standing on ground that might hold her in a few weeks. It was one of the most horrific days of my life. As we met with a funeral director, I explained that we would not be purchasing anything that day. We would be putting a plot on hold and would see if the Lord was going to choose for us to use it. The funeral director seemed a bit confused, and I doubt she hears this much. Usually, a cemetery isn't really "Plan B."

In this and many other circumstances, I had the opportunity to talk about my Jesus. Strangers wanted to know why I would make such a choice, and as I told them, I would see their faces as they tried to process what I was saying. It often led to more questions, and many times turned into a conversation that pushed them to think about their own mortality and the idea of eternity. Also, I prayed that they would come away valuing life.

As soon as Audrey was woven in my womb, she was a child. She was my child. And yet, she wasn't. She was God's all along, and I bowed down to that fact every day I carried her.

I decided to start writing a blog (*audreycaroline .blogspot.com*) to keep my friends and family updated, because telling the story over and over again overwhelmed me, and I thought it would be the easiest way to share what was going on. I had no idea that it would blossom into what it has, and I'm indebted to the many, many people who prayed with us as we walked through this terrible season.

As the weeks went by, the diagnosis changed slightly. There were certain things doctors had expected to see that

Audrey was inside me and she was alive, and yet I was standing on ground that might hold her in a few weeks.

they didn't. They also realized that Audrey had four chambers in her heart and that the organs they thought were missing were actually there. We felt like we had front-row seats to a miracle, and every day we prayed for our child to be well.

In the event that there was a memorial service, I wanted a song to be played that was written just for her. One day I sat down with Todd, who is the lead singer in the group Selah, and our friend Christa Wells and wrote a song called "I Will Carry You." A few weeks later, when we recorded it, I held the headphones over my stomach and felt Audrey Caroline scoot around as she listened. I cried, imagining that those little hiccups and elbows weren't going to be mine.

And yet, we never gave up hope. As hard as it was some days, we refused to surrender to a place where there was no hope. And before we knew it, the day had come to meet our daughter.

On April 7, 2008, we welcomed our sweet Audrey Caroline into this world. She had red hair and the nurses cooed over her as I begged Todd for details.

"Is she alive?"

"She's alive, honey. And she is beautiful." He was crying as he whispered to me.

I saw the nurses evaluating her and it seemed like they were taking a long time, so my mind began to wander. *Maybe we would take her home after all. Could it be?* I remember telling God that it wasn't too late. I stared at them, trying to make out anything from their hushed conversation.

A few moments later, I saw one of them remove her stethoscope. The others did the same, and quietly they left the room.

And so did my hope.

There wasn't going to be a miracle today. Not the one we wanted, at least. My doctor confirmed her diagnosis and told us that Audrey was alive but that her heart rate was slowing and she wasn't sure how long we would have with her. I cried as they laid our baby girl on my chest, and I told her she didn't have to stay for us. I told her that her Father was waiting for her. I stroked her head and breathed her in as tears came down my cheeks. I couldn't get enough of her

While Angie was carrying Audrey, the family visited Disney World, at daughter Ellie's request.

sweet little face, her eyes half-open and trying to assess the situation. As they took me back to my room, I introduced her to everyone we passed, never mentioning that she was sick. I was so proud to be her mommy for as long as the Lord would allow.

We know now that He allowed about 2½ hours. She passed away in my arms with all of her sisters sitting on the bed with me. It was a peaceful moment, one marked by the love of a family who believed that she was being welcomed into the arms of her Savior.

Shortly after that, we sat as a family around her tiny wooden coffin and the girls ripped the Band-Aids off Audrey's stuffed bunny and threw them into the wind.

Our Audrey-bunny was healed.

We miss her every day. I walk around the house, staring at the place where her crib was supposed to be. I wonder if she would have liked sweet potatoes, and what would have made her giggle. There are days when the pain is so intense I feel like I can't move, and others where a peace comes over me and I thank God for the respite.

If you are a woman who has walked this valley, I want you to know that your child matters. You don't need to "move on" and pretend he or she never happened, nor do you need to feel guilty for the pain you carry.

The truth is, our sweet baby girl probably brought more people to the Lord than I will in my lifetime. People wanted to know her story. When the name of Jesus came up, they were curious: Who is this God who gives me strength that defies the situation? God stirred so many hearts, and to this day we stand amazed at the legacy of a three-pound baby.

Since losing Audrey, I've been overwhelmed by the number of similar stories I've heard from women who lost children. I was shocked by how many women had never shared their story. There were several I met who had lost babies decades ago and hadn't spoken of it since. As we spoke and the tears filled their eyes, we knew that it wasn't an ache that was going to go away. The years pass and life continues, but the loss is ever-present.

I've learned so much about grief in the past few years, and the one thing I know is that it isn't a linear path. It doesn't seem to follow any logical pattern, and the only thing I know to do is to feel it. I don't stop myself from crying, nor do I avoid conversations with my children that are painful. I know that they miss Audrey Caroline too, and I want them to have the right to grieve. Sometimes they want to color pictures, and other times they just need to cry. I don't stop them from feeling, and I don't run from the hard questions. There have been times when I have said, "Honey, I just don't know the answer to that, but God does and we are just going to have to trust Him. It's really hard for me to do that too."

If you are a woman who has walked this valley, I want you to know that your child matters. You don't need to "move on" and pretend he or she never happened, nor do you need to feel guilty for the pain you carry. It's natural to feel a gaping hole that refuses to be filled — no matter how many years it has been or how many other children you may have. The Lord knows your pain, and as you seek Him, my prayer is that you will find rest in His presence. No matter what you are feeling, bring it to Him. He can handle your screaming at the top of your lungs or crying out in pain. He isn't intimidated by your questioning or your doubt. He longs to father you and for you to willingly share the depths of your grief with Him.

I can honestly say I've found solace in prayer and hope in God's Word. I know now that no matter what this life brings me, I only need Him to get through it. Before Audrey, I was so nervous, always wondering what might go wrong and worrying about all the possibilities. I'm learning slowly to take my hands from the wheel and sit back, breathe a sigh of relief, and give the Lord full reign.

My sweet Audrey, even now you are making me brave … we love you, precious girl … ☐

I Will Carry You

Angie Smith's book, *I Will Carry You: The Sacred Dance of Grief and Joy* (B&H), can be found at your local LifeWay Christian Store.

I Will Carry You tells the powerful story of a parent losing her child, interwoven with the biblical story of Lazarus, to help those who mourn to still have hope — to find grace and peace in the sacred dance of grief and joy.

Angie Smith *is the proud wife of Todd Smith (of the Christian group Selah), mother to four precious girls, and is expecting her fifth child. You can keep up with Angie on her blog, Bring the Rain (audreycaroline.blogspot.com).*

1. The people of God were doing all sorts of _____ _____.

2. Faith is taking God at _____ _____.

3. Resting in faith means we rest in the _____ of _____.

4. Are you gaining _____ with God?

5. We can run to Jesus, our High Priest, to find grace in our time of _____.

6. God's Word says _____ _____ are coming.

7. We must know His Word and then take His Word and live in the _____ of _____.

8. The rest of faith is _____ the Word of God with faith

for a particular _____.

GROUP DISCUSSION QUESTIONS

1. Ephesians 4:29 says, "Let no unwholesome word proceed from your mouth, but only such a word as is good for edification according to the need of the moment, so that it will give grace to those who hear." Share an example of heeding the advice of this verse and one of when you wish you had.

2. Discuss with your group about a time when you took a stand for Christ. How did God use that decision to help you mature in your faith?

WEEK TWO | DAY ONE
Inheriting the Promises

The Word of God overflows with promises to those who belong to Him. They are our inheritance as children of God. No wonder God both reminded the Hebrews that they inherited the promises through faith and patience, even as He warned them of the dangers of drifting away. God definitely gave them warnings to be heeded, yet God let the recipients of this letter know, "we are convinced of better things concerning you, and things that accompany salvation, though we are speaking in this way" (Heb. 6:9).

Good deeds, a Christlike walk, and a continuance in the faith, along with other changes, are the evidence of our salvation. True salvation transforms an individual for life, making that person a new creation in Christ Jesus (2 Cor. 5:17). Salvation washes, sanctifies, and justifies us. Paul told his readers to not be deceived if they were still living in their sins (1 Cor. 6:9-10).

In the video session we went from the end of Hebrews 5 to Hebrews 6:10-12, where we begin this week. However, before we go any further, please pray and ask God to exhort you through His Word today, to take His truth deep into your inner being, renewing you and strengthening you with His power.

> Read the verses below and as before color or underline the references to the people of this letter. Don't miss the *beloved!* Circle any reference to *time* ⏰. Mark *faith* with the symbol of the book ▱ as you marked the references to the Word in week 1. Remember, faith comes from hearing and hearing by the word of Christ (Rom. 10:17). That's why I mark *faith* the same way I mark the *Word.* But you do what is best for you!

Hebrews 6:9-12

⁹But, beloved, we are convinced of better things concerning you, and things that accompany salvation, though we are speaking in this way.

¹⁰For God is not unjust so as to forget your work and the love which you have shown toward His name, in having ministered and in still ministering to the saints.

¹¹And we desire that each one of you show the same diligence so as to realize the full assurance of hope until the end,

¹²so that you will not be sluggish, but imitators of those who through faith and patience inherit the promises.

List not only what you learn about the people, but also list any warning. At the close of Hebrews the author wrote, "But I urge you, brethren, bear with this word of exhortation, for I have written to you briefly" (13:22). Let's not miss the exhortations.

The Description   The Exhortation

As you observed this text, along with Hebrews 5:11–6:1 and 10:32-39, you've learned quite a bit about the "Hebrews." You've seen a "sluggishness" about them when it comes to their faith. Thus the warnings about listening and not drifting away (2:1), of holding fast (3:6,14), of pressing on to maturity (6:1).

The Christian life is not to be lived sloppily or casually, but diligently. *Diligence* is a word that is greatly lacking in the vocabulary of Americans today. The Greek word is *spoudés,* which comes from *speúd* meaning to "speed, urge, hasten, press." It's translated *speed, haste, earnestness, diligence, zeal.* In other words, it means you are to get with it.

According to Hebrews 6:9-12, what does diligence bring?

And how do you "inherit" the promises of God?

Did you write *faith and patience* as answer to that last question? Patience is *makrothymia* and carries the idea of self-restraint, long-suffering.

Are you, by any chance, a "now" gal? I am! "Oh let's go now!" "Let's do it now." Because of my strong teaching, strong personality, and passion, people who don't know me often wonder if I am any fun. I can assure you, I am! I love people, love to laugh, love to go. I love to do so many things. So I often have to restrain myself. In my flesh, if today is good, yesterday would have been even better! How thankful I am for the indwelling Spirit of God and the fruit He brings with Him. I desperately need His self-control

We live in a *now* generation. An *instant* world. Instant coffee, instant tea, instant oatmeal are OK, but when it comes to instant gratification of the flesh, that leads to all sorts of indulgences and immorality, doesn't it? Look at our culture, at the problems among those who profess Christ. Beloved, we cannot live that way. We must live by every word that comes from the mouth of our God and Father! And God doesn't always answer our prayers, supply our needs, heal our hurts instantly, does He?

What have you been waiting for, my friend? asking God for?

Now, examine it. Is it in accordance with the character of God, the will of God, the Word of God?

If the answer is no, it's not pleasing to God, then let it go. It's not good for you. If you got it, you would be sorry. You don't want God to give you the desire of your heart and send leanness to your soul (Ps. 106:15), do you?

However, if it's biblically OK—in accordance with the character of God, the will of God, the Word of God—then discuss it with Him in prayer. Stay in communication with Him as it comes to your mind and heart; walk in faith and patience. "Wait for the Lord" (Ps. 27:14).

See what God does, what He says, how He leads. And know this, if it is for your good and His glory, you will get it. That is His promise.

You may ask, "How do you know what God's promises are?"

I answer, once again only through diligence. First ask, Does it line up with His character, His will, His purpose? Let me take you to a verse you need to memorize. In Paul's last letter to Timothy, knowing he was going to die, Paul gave his son in the gospel numerous instructions. Many of them had to do with the Word of God that Timothy was to guard with his life as Paul had done, no matter the suffering (2 Tim. 1:8-14).

In 2 Timothy 2:15 Paul called Timothy to diligence. See the text below. As you observe it, underline the references to *Timothy*, put a box around *diligent*, and mark the reference to *God's Word* as you have before.

2 Timothy 2:15

15Be diligent to present yourself approved to God as workman who does not need to be ashamed, accurately handling the word of truth.

Now list what you learned about:

Timothy (what he was to be, to do)

The Word of God

The Hebrews were struggling because they had been sluggish in their faith rather than diligent. You and I will find ourselves in the same situation if we are not diligent!

O dear, daughter, I plead with you, listen to this older woman. Learn how to endure, to persevere, to live by every word that comes out of His mouth. Remember, without faith it is impossible to please God! You must believe He is God and that He is a rewarder of those who diligently seek Him (Heb. 11:6, KJV).

As we close today, make it your ambition to be pleasing to Him (2 Cor. 5:9).

God's Plan

Have you ever stopped to really consider what God intended for man and still does even though we sinned?

From the very beginning of the Book of Hebrews, the focus is on the Son of God. The truths of chapter 1 are breathtaking when you ponder their insights into this Son who is called God and whose throne is forever and ever. That a day will come when righteousness will reign supreme gives you hope in times like this. We live in the midst of what Philippians 2:15 calls "a crooked and perverse generation." We await the "world to come" (Heb. 2:5). This is the world, the kingdom and the King for whom we live! We must persevere in faith.

In Hebrews 2 God reminds us of what He intends for man. It is printed out below. The words in capitals are taken from Psalm 8. As you read it, underline every reference to *man*.

Hebrews 2:6-8

⁶But one has testified somewhere, saying,

"WHAT IS MAN, THAT YOU REMEMBER HIM? OR THE SON OF MAN, THAT YOU ARE CONCERNED ABOUT HIM?

⁷"YOU HAVE MADE HIM FOR A LITTLE WHILE LOWER THAN THE ANGELS; YOU HAVE CROWNED HIM WITH GLORY AND HONOR, AND HAVE APPOINTED HIM OVER THE WORKS OF YOUR HANDS;

⁸YOU HAVE PUT ALL THINGS IN SUBJECTION UNDER HIS FEET."

For in subjecting all things to him, He left nothing that is not subject to him. But now we do not yet see all things subjected to him.

Now, diligent student, list below what you learn from marking the references to man.

Some people too quickly assume this is a prophecy about Jesus, but when you carefully observe the text, you see this is God's intention for mankind. Man's sin sidetracked God's plan for man *but* it didn't thwart it. Jesus, our Redeemer, was in the shadows.

Now read the next two verses, Hebrews 2:9-11. Mark the references to *Jesus* as you did previously with a cross †, red if you have it. Mark the pronouns and the synonyms that refer to Jesus such as "author." As you do your observations, note that some pronouns such as "Him" and "whom" in verse 10 refer to God the Father. Watch for these, but don't mark them (unless you mark them in another way). You can tell who is who by reading the verses carefully. Underline the references to those who are *sanctified* and thus *believers*.

Hebrews 2:9-11

⁹But we do see Him who was made for a little while lower than the angels, namely, Jesus, because of the suffering of death crowned with glory and honor, so that by the grace of God He might taste death for everyone. ¹⁰For it was fitting for Him, for whom are all things, and through whom are all things, in bringing many sons to glory, to perfect the author of their salvation through sufferings. ¹¹For both He who sanctifies and those who are sanctified are all from one Father, for which reason He is not ashamed to call them brethren.

Once again, list below what your God is telling you about His Son. List what you learn about those who become sons (children of God, sanctified). Remember this isn't busy work; it is studying, hanging on God's every word! I am giving you more space than you need because we will add to this list in just a few minutes.

Jesus   Sons of God (Sanctified)

Now read through Hebrews 2:14-15 and do the following: Underline every reference to *believers*. Mark every reference to *Jesus,* and put three dots in the form of a triangle over *therefore*. "Therefore" is a term of conclusion. So see what "therefore" is there for!

Hebrews 2:14-15

¹⁴Therefore, since the children share in flesh and blood, He Himself likewise also partook of the same, that through death He might render powerless him who had the power of death, that is, the devil, ¹⁵and might free those who through fear of death were subject to slavery all their lives.

Add what you learned from marking *Jesus* to the list under Jesus. What did you learn about believers from these verses? List those in the column marked Sons of God (Sanctified).

There is more to see, beloved, on the subject of the death of Jesus. We will look at that tomorrow. I just want you to know that what you are going to see is so wonderful—truths filled with wonder! Liberating truth!

I want to bring today to a close by asking you two things. First, think about what you've learned about Jesus, the Son of God today. What touches you the most and why? Write it out below, or highlight it in some way on the list on the previous page. Then spend some time in worship. To worship is to look at someone's worth, to bow before Him.

Second, did you realize what God has in store for you, as a human being, whom He has redeemed from sin and brought into His family? Look at the list you've recorded and write a prayer to God the Father and God the Son expressing your gratitude for so great a salvation. Let God the Spirit within lead you into praise and thanksgiving as you enter His courts.

The Necessary Sacrifice

Hebrews 2:14-15

[14]Therefore, since the children share in flesh and blood, He Himself likewise also partook of the same, that through death He [15]might render powerless him who had the power of death, that is, the devil, and might free those who through fear of death were subject to slavery all their lives.

Did you see it—"subject to slavery all their lives?" I was there until I was 29—a slave. I remember when God convicted me of my sin, of my quest for love that drove me from one man to another. I knew it was wrong, and I told Him I would stop. But I didn't. The Bible says whoever sins is the slave of sin (John 8:34). In the words of today, sin is addictive.

Today we study how we can be set free. If you don't need these truths for yourself, someone you know needs them. Study well so you can show them truth.

Look back to Hebrews 2:14-15 above, and we'll let Scripture interpret Scripture by going to a portion of Hebrews 10 we haven't looked at yet. Please read Hebrews 2:14-15 aloud so that you not only see but hear truth.

As the text tells us and as you saw yesterday, Jesus became man because we are man. He who is God and who has always been God, one with the Father, became man. It is called the "incarnation"—*carne* being flesh. Jesus purposefully did this because only man can pay for man's sins. But not just any man. Why?

> Look up Romans 3:9,23 in your Bible and record what the verses teach about mankind.

> Man is born in sin. And what is the sinner's fate? his destiny? Look up these verses in your Bible and write down what you learn. I am having you go to your Bible so that you know where these verses are and can share them with others.

> Romans 5:12

> Romans 6:23

Death is the fate, the destiny, of sinners. God does not revoke His Word. He told Adam that if he and Eve ate of the fruit of the tree of the knowledge of good and evil, they would surely die. And die they did! Sin entered the world and with it death. Adam and Eve reproduced after their kind, giving birth to sinners.

The Devil had the power of death over man because of the sin of man. But if man's sin can be taken care of, paid for in a way that satisfies (propitiates) the holiness of God, then the Devil's power is broken.

Let's fast forward for a few minutes to Hebrews 10. We are going to look at some key verses that will enrich our understanding of Hebrews 2:14-15.

In Hebrews 10:1-5,9-10, mark the following in a distinctive way or color: References to *sacrifices.* These were required in the Old Testament to cover a person's sin. Be sure to mark synonymous phrases the same way such as "the blood of bulls and goats." References to *sin* I normally color brown. References to *Jesus.*

Hebrews 10:1-5,9-10

¹For the Law, since it has only a shadow of the good things to come and not the very form of things, can never, by the same sacrifices which they offer continually year by year, make perfect those who draw near.
²Otherwise, would they not have ceased to be offered, because the worshipers, having once been cleansed, would no longer have had consciousness of sins?
³But in those sacrifices there is a reminder of sins year by year.
⁴For it is impossible for the blood of bulls and goats to take away sins.
⁵Therefore, when He comes into the world, He says, "SACRIFICE AND OFFERING YOU HAVE NOT DESIRED, BUT A BODY YOU HAVE PREPARED FOR ME.
⁹then He said, "BEHOLD, I HAVE COME TO DO YOUR WILL." He takes away the first in order to establish the second.
¹⁰By this will we have been sanctified through the offering of the body of Jesus Christ once for all.

Now list what you learn from marking the three key words:

Sacrifices   Sin   He (Jesus)

The blood of animals cannot pay for man's sins; only the death of a sinless man can. And who, beloved, is that sinless man? And why is He sinless? Because He was conceived of the Spirit and placed in the virgin's womb. Jesus was the last Adam (1 Cor. 15:45-47). Though tempted as was the first Adam, Jesus did not sin.

Did you see the parallel with Hebrews 2:14? Jesus took on a body; He became a human being. Because you and I are flesh and blood, He became the same so that He might taste death for you—die in your place, be made sin for you.

And what was the result of Jesus' death? What did He accomplish? Read the following verses from Hebrews 10 and mark the references to *Jesus;* the references to *sacrifice, offering;* the references to *sin*; and the references to "those who are sanctified"—*those, them, their.*

Hebrews 10:12,14-18

¹²but He, having offered one sacrifice for sins for all time, SAT DOWN AT THE RIGHT HAND OF GOD ...
¹⁴For by one offering He has perfected for all time those who are sanctified.
¹⁵And the Holy Spirit also testifies to us; for after saying,

¹⁶"THIS IS THE COVENANT THAT I WILL MAKE WITH THEM AFTER THOSE DAYS, SAYS THE LORD: I WILL PUT MY LAWS UPON THEIR HEART, AND ON THEIR MIND I WILL WRITE THEM,"
He then says,
¹⁷"AND THEIR SINS AND THEIR LAWLESS DEEDS I WILL REMEMBER NO MORE."
¹⁸Now where there is forgiveness of these things, there is no longer any offering for sin.

Let's see what you learned from these verses. List your insights:

Jesus   Those Who Are Sanctified

If you, as a child of God, are moaning and groaning about your sins, about your B.C. days (before you came to know the Christ), your past, what does that say to God? What does that tell you about your faith?

If you are focused on your past sin, is what you are doing pleasing to God? Why or why not?

Jesus paid it all! You cannot pay a thing! His sacrifice was sufficient. Your sins are remembered no more by Him. Why are you remembering them? You are forgiven! I want to shout it, don't you? I AM FORGIVEN FOREVER AND EVER!

Don't you ever say, "But I cannot forgive myself!" You don't need to forgive yourself. Nothing is biblical about that statement. It's a hiss from the serpent of old, the Devil himself, to put your focus on yourself rather than God. You confess your sin, God forgives, and that is it!

You need to believe God. This is how the righteous person lives. To not believe is a lack of faith, and that does not please God. What more can God do? He gave His Son for you! What more can He say? Through one offering Jesus has perfected us for forever. The whole Bible takes us to this moment—the crucifixion of Jesus Christ, His death for your life.

"Through His own blood, He entered the holy place once for all, having obtained eternal redemption" (Heb. 9:12) for *you*. Come running to the throne of God, the mercy seat when sin troubles your heart and mind. The mercy seat covered the ark of the covenant that held the tablets of the 10 commandments. It was where the blood of a goat was put on the day of atonement, once a year. The ark and the mercy seat represented the throne of God.

Read through the following verses from Hebrews 10:19-23. Mark every reference to the *brethren* (believers) including "we," "us," "our," and mark every reference to *Jesus*.

¹⁹Therefore, brethren, since we have confidence to enter the holy place by the blood of Jesus,

²⁰by a new and living way which He inaugurated for us through the veil, that is, His flesh,

²¹and since we have a great priest over the house of God,

²²let us draw near with a sincere heart in full assurance of faith, having our hearts sprinkled clean from an evil conscience and our bodies washed with pure water.

²³Let us hold fast the confession of our hope without wavering, for He who promised is faithful;

Once again list what you learn from marking Jesus and those who are the brethren.

Jesus   The Brethren

Now, beloved, I must ask you if you have come to the mercy seat. Have you told God of your sins, of your helplessness to free yourself from their slavery? Have you cried out to Him for deliverance?

Have you believed that Jesus is the Son of God—man in the flesh without sin? the Lamb of God who alone can take away your sins? the Son of God who went to the cross to become sin *for you* that *you* might be forgiven forever and receive the gift of eternal life so that *you* might become His child, be born again into God's forever family?

If not, are you ready to believe and be set free from sin and death? to become a true child of God? If so, write your prayer to God and date it! It's your birthday, and I welcome you to the family of God.

Finally, dear one, if you have time bring today to a close by meditating on some verses from your Bible. Ponder Hebrews 9:3-7 and then 2:17 until they well up in your being and you are filled to the full with thanksgiving for your great High Priest for so great a salvation.

If you don't have the CD *Travis Cotttell: Jesus Saves Live,* I urge you to get it and use it to worship the Lord. The song "Mercy Seat" featuring Angela Cruz bids you to "come running to the mercy seat." If you're leading a group, you'll want to play it for the class after the video teaching. If you can, read Hebrews 8; 9; and 10 before and you'll appreciate it even more.

The Rest of Faith

Life is becoming more and more difficult, isn't it? Stressful. Uncertain. Shaky, to say the least. How are you going to handle it? How are you going to function? to walk in such a way that through faith and patience you inherit the promises?

You do it, dear child of God, by the "rest" of faith. You can do it. You have High Priest who also was tempted yet endured. No matter what comes your way, you and I can live as God would have us live because we have Jesus. He is our very present help for every situation of life; and because He lives within, He brings with Him the surpassing greatness of His power.

Return to Hebrews 2 and look again at the verses that bring this chapter to a close, leading us into Hebrews 3 and 4 where we see the "rest" of faith.

> Begin with Hebrews 2:16-18. Mark the pronouns for *Jesus,*
> starting with the first "He." Mark the references to being *tempted.*

Hebrews 2:16-18

16For assuredly He does not give help to angels, but He gives help to the descendant of Abraham.

17Therefore, He had to be made like His brethren in all things, so that He might become a merciful and faithful high priest in things pertaining to God, to make propitiation for the sins of the people.

18For since He Himself was tempted in that which He has suffered, He is able to come to the aid of those who are tempted.

> What did you learn from marking *Jesus*?

> What is Jesus able to do for you when you are tempted?

Stop for a moment and think about the last time you were tempted to take a path or respond in a way that wasn't in line with the Word of God or the character of God who calls us to Christlikeness.

> What did you do when you found yourself being tempted?

Was this the way you usually handle temptation? When you find yourself being tempted, what do you usually do?

I remember years ago when we were taking a teaching tour to Israel. It was in the earlier days when we used an agency run by a very handsome Arab man. I was much younger, and, of course, I've already shared my past.

While on the trip I ended up with a cyst in my ear that had to be excised before I could ever get on a plane. So our Arab friend picked me up at the hotel. As we walked out the door, we encountered some of his friends entering the hotel. I couldn't understand a word they said, but I knew …

It was an exquisite day, flowers in bloom, sweetly filling the air with their perfumes, puffy clouds drifting lazily through the soft blue of the sky. Ever a gentlemen, my Arab guide opened the door and I got in. When he slid behind the wheel, he put his arm on the back of the seat, leaned toward me smiling winsomely, dark brown eyes twinkling. "The friends we just passed were kidding me about being out with you."

At that moment and in that setting, everything in my flesh wanted to flirt with him—nothing more, just flirt as I did in days of old. To feel like a carefree girl again, delighting in the enchantment of the encounter.

But with the temptation came the battle, my flesh would not go unopposed for the Spirit of God lived within. He came in when I came to Christ. I knew what was happening and I knew that my Arab friend professed Jesus but didn't possess him. I knew I was to witness, not flirt! We often think we can do both. What deception that idea is.

Witness I did!

Later that day I stood in the garden of Gethsemane next to an olive tree as old as the night Jesus wrestled with the will of God. As I taught our group, I came to our Lord's words to the three disciples Jesus asked to keep watch with Him, "So you men could not keep watch with Me for one hour? Keep watching and praying that you may not enter into temptation; the spirit is willing but the flesh is weak" (Matt. 26:40-41).

The words would barely come. I was overwhelmed. Weeping. Fighting the sobs that wanted to burst out of my being. For the first time the truth of what Jesus experienced pierced my heart, illumined my understanding.

Jesus understood the weakness of the flesh. Hadn't He gone to the Father in great agony, sweating blood, asking the Father that if it were possible to "let this cup pass from Me"? He didn't pray it once, or twice, but three times.

I have a High Priest who truly can be touched with my weaknesses, one tempted in all ways as we are. And because of that, as Hebrews 2:16 says, He is able to help me as He promises to the descendant (seed) of Abraham. "If you belong to Christ, then you are Abraham's descendents, heirs according to promise" (Gal. 3:29).

"Therefore, holy brethren, partakers of a heavenly calling, consider Jesus, the Apostle and High Priest of our confession" (Heb. 3:1). He was faithful, and you and I and every single child of God are to be faithful. Since He Himself was tempted in that which He suffered, He is able to come to the aid of those who are tempted (Heb. 2:18).

O beloved, as I write this, I have to ask you, Is your heart burning as mine is with the desire to be faithful, to listen carefully to Him, His Word? If it is, why don't you pause for a minute and pour out your desire even as I have just done?

The Hebrews were being tempted, tried, tested, and they were warned not to drift away from what God had said through His Son (2:1). In Hebrews 3 He again warns them. Let's read it.

> As you read, underline "you" and "your" as it is a direct reference to the recipients. Mark the references to the people from the past that He uses as an illustration: "they," "fathers," "generation." If you don't have a color, you can simply put a check over them (since they've checked out and are in heaven now!). Mark "rest."

Hebrews 3:7-11

[7]Therefore, just as the Holy Spirit says,
"Today if you hear His voice,
"Today if you hear His voice,
[8]Do not harden your hearts as when they provoked Me,
 as in the day of trial in the wilderness,
[9]Where your fathers tried Me by testing Me,
 And saw My works for forty years.
[10]"Therefore i was angry with this generation,
 And said, "They always go astray in their heart,
 And they did not know My ways';
[11]As i swore in My wrath, 'They shall not enter My rest.'"

> What did you learn from marking the following? List your insights.
>
> The "You and Your"   The Generations of the Past

The "rest" that God referred to is the land God promised to Abraham, Isaac, and Jacob as an everlasting possession. While we don't have time to study this chapter verse by verse, let me take you to Hebrews 3:17–4:3 where once again this rest is mentioned. As you read these verses, keep in mind what we saw in Hebrews 6:12 when we talked of sluggishness. Through faith and patience we inherit the promises. Contrast that with the verses that follow.

> As you read, mark the references to "rest." Mark "believe" and "unbelief" both the same way and then put a / over "unbelief."

[17]And with whom was He angry for forty years? Was it not with those who sinned, whose bodies fell in the wilderness?

[18]And to whom did He swear that they would not enter His rest, but to those who were disobedient?

[19]So we see that they were not able to enter because of unbelief.

[4:1]Therefore, let us fear if, while a promise remains of entering His rest, any one of you may seem to have come short of it.

[2]For indeed we have had good news preached to us, just as they also; but the word they heard did not profit them, because it was not united by faith in those who heard.

[3]For we who have believed enter that rest, just as He has said,

If you have time, you would find it so enlightening to read Numbers 13 and 14 and observe what happened with the children of Israel after 10 of the 12 spies brought back a bad report about the land God promised to Abraham, Isaac, and Jacob. This is the incident the author of Hebrews was referring to.

What is so sad is that instead of believing and trusting God to stand by His Word, they threw a tantrum of unbelief that cost them 40 years of wandering in the wilderness and the lives of those who died in the wilderness during that 40 years. Only Joshua and Caleb were spared, and that is because they were the two spies who believed God.

Listen to Caleb when the people were panicked by the words of men who were ignoring the Word of God because of what they had seen: "We should by all means go up and take possession of it, for we will surely overcome it" (Num. 13:30).

This, beloved, is the rest of faith! Let me give you my definition of the rest of faith and then you can see if it holds biblically. You heard it in my message:

Rest is uniting the Word with faith and living in it at that very moment. It's the action of faith for today—for this moment, this situation. If I were going to give you a visual of the rest of faith, it would be your head resting on the Bible.

When you marked "rest," "believed," and "unbelief," did you see that definition at work, beloved?

Draw an arrow from "unbelief" in verse 19 to "disobedient" in verse 18, and you will see the root of disobedience: unbelief.

Unbelief is a lack of faith! And that is sin. "Whatever is not from faith is sin" (Rom. 14:23). That is what God called it in Hebrews 3:17. Mark "sinned" (I color it brown). Then read Hebrews 3:17-19 aloud. Hear His words of truth.

Now look at 4:1. What does it begin with and what is significant about this word?

Did you mark "it" in 4:1 as you marked "rest"? If not, do it as the "it" is rest!

Now read 4:2 and mark the word "faith."

Do you see it, dear one? The Word of God must be united with faith! To know God's Word is one thing, but to live by it, apply it, trust it, act on it, cling to it, that is another thing altogether.

Read Hebrews 4:3 aloud: "We who have believed enter that rest."

When you believe—put action to His truth—you enter His rest. And that enables you to inherit His promises, to receive the full benefit of faith, and to please God.

Now, beloved, is there something in your life that you need to apply this truth to? Can you briefly write it down?

According to God's Word, how are you to believe, to obey? Remember obedience is synonymous with believing.

Will you obey? Will you rest? Will you unite God's Word with faith and live accordingly?

If not, what will you do?

Will You Believe?

We are living in epochal times. Our faith is going to be tried and tested to the core. We have a decision to make. Will we go with Jesus, despised and rejected of men, outside the gate? Will we grab onto the Word of God and determine before God Almighty that we are going to grow up? to go on to maturity?

If God has spoken, what an awful, shame it will be to us if we don't listen. What a shame if we do not make the effort to study His Word and make Him our number one priority. He is God, and He is to have first place in all things!

We are to deny ourselves and take up our cross and go out with Him bearing His reproach. We have nothing here that will last, but we have a city to come whose builder and architect is God. We are to persevere until the trumpet sounds and the dead in Christ are raised (1 Thess. 4:16).

May we fix our eyes on Jesus, the author and perfecter of our faith!

What does faith look like in the eyes of God? God tells us right after Hebrews 10:35-39, where He exhorted the recipients of Hebrews to not throw away their confidence but to endure, to live by faith.

Hebrews 11 is an incredible chapter, the "hall of faith" that displays the heroes of the ages. "By faith" is a key repeated phrase in this chapter, but before that repeated phrase is introduced, there is the verse that says, "Now faith is....

Hebrews 11:1-2

[1]Faith is the assurance of things hoped for, the conviction of things not seen. [2]For by it the men of old gained approval.

> Read the text again, aloud and mark "faith" and its pronoun as you have before. Faith is two things. Write them below. "Assurance" can also be translated *substance* and "conviction" translated *evidence*.

> 1.

> 2.

> According to what you have learned this past two weeks, why does faith gain approval?

> Read Romans 10:17 in your Bible. What does it say?

We will look at portions of Hebrews 11 to learn how people lives by faith in their varied life circumstances. In the verses that follow remember what faith *is* and watch how it is lived out. We begin where God starts in the demonstration of faith because it is primary, foundational, and controversial in our culture. It is something you must deal with if you are going to be strong in your faith.

Read Hebrews 11:3 below. Mark "by faith." Underline the references to the author/recipients.

³By faith we understand that the worlds were prepared by the word of God, so that what is seen was not made out of things which are visible.

Why is this verse controversial? What is it saying?

Can you include yourself in the "we"? Why?

God began His Bible with the creation by His Word. He spoke and it was so. Throughout the Word of God He confirmed this over and over. You saw it in Hebrews 1:10. Jesus was there and active in creation, as John 1:1-2 also tells us.

Are you going to believe it? It is a matter of faith. No one was there but God the Father, Son, and Spirit when the world, plants, creatures, and man were created. Yet many in the world say that isn't the way it was. They weren't there, but they have their theories. Beloved, that is all they are! Just theories.

So your first act of faith: Are you going to believe God's book? When you study the Bible, you'll observe God reminding His people every time they face challenges and difficulties that He is the Creator; therefore, nothing is too difficult for Him! Why? He wanted them to live by faith, not the fear of man!

Now, the word of faith is in your court. What will you do with it? Remember Hebrews 11:6: "Without faith it is impossible to please Him, for he who comes to God must believe that He is and that He is a rewarder of those who seek Him."

Will you believe what God said about creation just as He wrote it? without editing Him? Write out your answer.

You need to see something that will help you keep your focus no matter what the days bring. Read Hebrews 11:3-16 from your Bible. As you read mark "by faith" or any occurrence of faith. Write in the margin the name of each person being used as an example.

It's inspiring to think of these people and how they lived. They didn't even have what you and I have—the privilege of living on this side of the cross, of having the Father, Son, and the Spirit make their home in us (John 14:17,23).

Read Hebrews 11:9-16 again and mark "promise" with a diamond shape like this ◊ or give it a color. Be sure to mark the pronouns "city" and "country."

Do you remember what we saw in Hebrews 6:11-12? If not, look it up in your Bible and mark it.

> Hebrews 6:12 says we are to be imitators of those who through
> faith and patience inherit the promises. What is the ultimate
> promise? What did you see marking "city" and "country"?

Have you ever studied Revelation 21 and 22? A new city, a new Jerusalem—this is our promise. This is part of our inheritance that comes through faith and patience. This is what Abraham, Sarah, Isaac, and others were looking for—waiting for in faith—a heavenly country that is far better. Remember in Hebrews 2:5 God spoke of the world to come.

All this makes me think of 2 Corinthians 4:17-18: "For momentary, light affliction is producing for us an eternal weight of glory far beyond all comparison, while we look not at the things which are seen, but at the things which are not seen (remember faith is the conviction of things not seen); for the things which are seen are temporal, but the things which are not seen are eternal."

It is very hard for me, precious student, to skip over the rest of Hebrews 11 to the last verses, but we must. Let's see how Hebrews 11 closes and flows into the first 3 verses of Hebrews 12.

> Read the verses and mark those key words we've been marking
> since we began: "faith," "promised," "sin," and of course, "Jesus."
> Also underline "endurance" and "endure."

Hebrews 11:39-12:3

39 And all these, having gained approval through their faith, did not receive what was promised,

40 because God had provided something better for us, so that apart from us they would not be made perfect.

12:1 Therefore, since we have so great a cloud of witnesses surrounding us, let us also lay aside every encumbrance and the sin which so easily entangles us, and let us run with endurance the race that is set before us,

2 fixing our eyes on Jesus, the author and perfecter of faith, who for the joy set before Him endured the cross, despising the shame, and has sat down at the right hand of the throne of God.

3 For consider Him who has endured such hostility by sinners against Himself, so that you will not grow weary and lose heart.

Did you notice the words *perfect* and *perfecter*? Go a little deeper and look at the meaning of this word in Greek. The word *perfect* is *teleió*; complete, mature. It means to complete, make perfect by reaching the intended goal. Jesus is referred to as the author and perfecter of faith.

Perfecter is a masculine noun from *teleió*. Thus He is the completer, the perfecter, of faith which reaches the goal so as to win the prize.

Author is *archegós*; a masculine noun from *arché*, beginning or rule, and *ág*, to lead. Beloved, Jesus therefore is the beginning, the first cause of faith, the Originator, founder, leader, chief, first, prince, as distinguished from simply being the cause. Jesus Christ is called the *archegós* of life (Acts 3:15) because He is *arché,* the beginning or the originator of God's creation (Rev. 3:14). Don't forget what you saw in Hebrews 11:3!

Compare this with Hebrews 2:10: "For it was fitting for Him (God) for whom are all things, in bringing many sons to glory, to perfect the author of their salvation through sufferings." Our author was perfected, matured, made complete through sufferings in order to bring us to glory.

The word *to fix your eyes* is *aphoráo.* It means to look; to look away steadfastly or intently toward a distant object. Metaphorically, to behold in the mind, to fix the mind upon (Phil. 2:23; Heb. 12:2).[1]

As we live this life of faith, we are to fix our mind on Jesus at all times. Oh how I long to remember this, to do it, to be cognizant of Jesus in everything.

Faith is a way of life. That is what Hebrews 11 teaches. It is the way we are to live. And do it we can! Look at the great cloud of witnesses simply mentioned in Hebrews 11, and then think of WHO we have as the author and perfecter of our faith. We have Jesus.

And where is He? What is He doing? He is seated at God's right hand. Your High Priest has finished His work of redemption. Your sins have been paid for once and for all by His sacrifice, by His blood. You have forgiveness of sins. You have Jesus , who holds His priesthood permanently. "Therefore He is able also to save forever those who draw near to God through Him, since He always lives to make intercession for them" (Heb. 7:24-25) for us. Now do you know why I call you precious?

Let us therefore fix our eyes on Him, beloved, even in the midst of the greatest of trials and suffering. No matter what the times bring, let us not grow weary and lose heart. Let us endure. Persevere.

Let us walk in faith and not "refuse Him who is speaking" (Heb. 12:25). With salvation in Jesus Christ, under the New Covenant in His blood, you and I have received a kingdom that cannot be shaken. And although He is about to shake the things that can be shaken (v. 26), we are to show gratitude by which we—all of us who profess Christ—may offer to our precious God and Father an acceptable service with reverence and awe (v. 28).

So now in the light of all you've learned, precious child of God, let's you and I "go out to Him outside the camp, bearing His reproach. For here we do not have a lasting city, but we are seeking the city which is to come" (Heb. 13:13-14).

Hebrews 13:20-22

[20]Now the God of peace, who brought up from the dead the great Shepherd of the sheep through the blood of the eternal covenant, even Jesus our Lord,

[21]equip you in every good thing to do His will, working in us that which is pleasing in His sight, through Jesus Christ, to whom be the glory forever and ever. Amen.

[22]But I urge you, brethren, bear with this word of exhortation, for I have written to you briefly.

---

1. S. Zodhiates, (2000, c1992, c1993). *The Complete Word Study Dictionary : New Testament* (electronic ed.) (G5048). Chattanooga, TN: AMG Publishers.

ABUNDANT

PRISCILLASHIRER

VIEWERGUIDE

Our God is _____!

God is able to _____ you.

One of the most fantastic attributes of God is simply that _____ _____.

The Book of Ephesians is considered by commentators to be the _____ of Paul's writings.

Ephesians 3:20-21

If you don't believe God is able, it will alter the way you _____.

SEVEN PRINCIPLES IN EPHESIANS 3:20-21

1. _____

_____ is the time to start considering the ability of God.

The two verses in Ephesians 3:20-21 are called a _____.

A doxology is an outpouring of _____, worship, and _____ to God.

John 10:10

The abundant life is when, in the midst of your _____ situation, you say, "Now is the time!"

2. _____

Hebrews 12:2

GROUP DISCUSSION QUESTIONS

1. Priscilla said God does not want us placing our hope or identity in anything other than our personal relationship with Him. How do you place your hope and identity in God?

2. Abundance really means pouring out honor, praise, and worship in spite of difficult circumstances. Can you share about a recent season of abundance in your life with your group members?

WEEK THREE | DAY ONE
Foundational Issues

The terminology the apostle Paul used in Ephesians applies to us as believers. When you feel down or insignificant, be refreshed by these words:
- "every spiritual blessing has been freely bestowed on us"
- "according to the riches of His grace which He lavished on us"
- "we have obtained a great inheritance"
- "the riches of the glory of His inheritance"
- "the surpassing greatness of His power toward us"

That's some good language, isn't it? It gets me excited when I think about the treasure our Savior made available to believers.

Why do you think we need a good foundational understanding of the riches God offers us as believers?

How might that understanding affect our confidence of trusting His ability to abundantly supply all our needs?

How does the wording used in those five promises speak of abundance rather than partial blessings?

Which of the five promises do you most struggle to believe? Why?

Which of the five promises do you embrace the easiest? Why?

In our video session I told about my misadventure with a flowerbed. I tried to grow flowers in defective soil. I began with a bad foundation. That story pictures multitudes of frustrated believers who are watering, fertilizing, and doing what they think should be necessary to make them grow spiritually, but they aren't seeing results. Many of those exhausted Christians may not have settled the foundational issue of what they believe about God. And you can't get more foundational than this—He is able.

Have you ever exhausted yourself because you were not fully embracing God's ability to work in your circumstances? If so, how?

How would you describe the current health of your spiritual soil?

Malnourished   Average   Healthy   Above Average   Excellent

Why would you describe your spiritual soil that way?

What measures are you currently taking to enhance the richness of your spiritual foundation? Pat yourself on the back for doing the work you are right now.

As in the story of the flowerbed, has there ever been a time in your life when you attempted to build upon a poor spiritual foundation and failed? If so, what did you learn?

Sister, your foundation is critical to your spiritual growth, and it is composed of what you believe to be true about God. I'm here to tell you that if you've not settled the question of God's ability, then you're going to find some things not happening in your spiritual life that you thought should be happening. Your foundation is what you believe about God. As we study together, take inventory of what you truly believe about Him.

In seminary one of the things we studied was systematic theology—the detailed, orderly exploration of what the Bible teaches about God. To understand the idea of systematic theology, imagine a human example. Think of your man if you are blessed or afflicted with one. He's so tall, he weighs so much, behaviorally you could describe the kinds of things he does. You could write an orderly exploration of what he is like. The result would be what you believe about him—sort of a "systematic man-ology." Or would that be "he-ology"?

I won't ask you to write such a description of some man, but I do want to ask you to think about who God is. What is God like? What can He do? What does He do? How does He act?

If you were writing an orderly explanation of what you believe about God, what six words or phrases you would list?

1.   4.

2.   5.

3.   6.

How does your daily life reflect that you actually believe the six descriptions you just wrote about God?

Which attributes of God listed in your description do you struggle to live like you believe in your daily walk with Him?

Which attributes of God listed in your description do you find easiest to demonstrate that you believe?

Rather than simply knowing things about God in theory, we need to know experientially whether or not He is trustworthy and faithful. Unless we are convinced that His character is trustworthy, we may be tempted to doubt either His ability or His willingness to meet our needs.

How do the following Scripture passages each speak to the faithfulness and trustworthy nature of God?

Deuteronomy 32:4

1 Chronicles 16:25-27

Psalm 33:4

Psalm 36:5

Ephesians 3:20-21

Which of the passages speaks most powerfully to you about God's faithfulness? Why?

How have you experienced God's faithfulness in a way described in this passage?

Have you ever allowed the unfaithfulness of other people to affect the way you perceive God's faithfulness? How?

Why is it so important that we look only to Scripture and not to other people when determining our stance on the faithfulness of God?

As you go through these weeks of study, allow the Lord to refresh your foundation. Ask Him to clearly reveal to you anything that needs to be dug up and replaced. Allowing Him to do a major overhaul will result in the growth we all need and desire.

Now

God has a time for you to start internalizing these precious truths and living like you believe and trust Him. The time is now.

Why do you think people often postpone trusting God's ability when they are in tough circumstances?

What are some of your most common excuses for not depending on God to handle your concerns?

How often do you get to the end of a day and realize that you spent more time trying hectically to handle your own circumstances rather than trusting God to take care of them?

☐ rarely   ☐ sometimes   ☐ often   ☐ constantly

Circle the phrases that best describe how you feel when trying to carry and control your own needs.
exhausted
overwhelmed
ill-equipped
unable
other_____

How might failing to recognize how quickly time passes lead someone to postpone investing in her spiritual life?

Why do you think Satan would love to convince us all that we have the capacity to take care of our own needs?

Look at some of the verses in Scripture that speak about time and our call to pursue God. Underline words or phrases in each that remind you of the importance to start believing His promises now.

2 Corinthians 6:2
In the time of my favor I heard you, and in the day of salvation I helped you. I tell you, now is the time of God's favor, now is the day of salvation.

Psalm 8:1-4
[1]O Lord, our Lord,
        how majestic is your name in all the earth!
  You have set your glory
        above the heavens.
[2]From the lips of children and infants
        you have ordained praise
  because of your enemies,
        to silence the foe and the avenger.
[3]When I consider your heavens,
        the work of your fingers,
  the moon and the stars,
        which you have set in place,
[4]what is man that you are mindful of him,
        the son of man that you care for him?

Galatians 6:7
Do not be deceived: God cannot be mocked. A man reaps what he sows.

Hebrews 4:7
Therefore God again set a certain day, calling it Today, when a long time later he spoke through David, as was said before:
    "Today, if you hear his voice,
      do not harden your hearts."

Romans 14:11
It is written:
    "'As surely as I live,' says the Lord,
    'every knee will bow before me;
        every tongue will confess to God.' "

If you were to list the reasons you should act or not act on God's Word now, what would your list look like? Take a few minutes to honestly and objectively consider what God is calling you to do right now, and write down the things that stand in the way of your acting. Then write about why you should act without delay.

My reasons to delay acting on God's Word to me include …

The reasons why I should obey God's command are …

If I obey, I risk the following results …

If I delay, I risk the following results …

What does the expression "delayed obedience is disobedience" mean to you?

The famous preacher Charles Spurgeon said of obedience: "Surely, though we have had to mourn our disobedience with many tears and sighs, we now find joy in yielding ourselves as servants of the Lord: our deepest desire is to do the Lord's will in all things. Oh, for obedience! It has been supposed by many ill-instructed people that the doctrine of justification by faith is opposed to the teaching of good works, or obedience. There is no truth in the supposition. We preach the obedience of faith."[1]

Can you, like so many of us, describe a time when you decided to obey God but chose not to do so immediately? If so, please share.

Have you ever intended to give something to God but just not right then? What happened?

Many experience the desire to follow God in a specific action only to have their desire swallowed up by laziness, greed, or fear. The Holy Spirit-inspired action remains undone because we delayed in its immediate application.

Merely *desiring* to do something for the Lord and actually *doing* something are two very different things. Latent and unfulfilled desires may either result in disobedience or a hindrance to our walk with the Lord.

When we delay acting on a desire, how do we decrease our chances of actually doing anything?

Use Galatians 6:7 and Hebrews 4:7 to write a personal challenge to yourself to begin acting immediately on the desires God grants you through His Word.

Talk with God about your challenge. Ask Him to give you the desire and the power (see Phil. 2:13) to live out the challenge.

Whatever God has asked you to pursue, He will accompany you to complete. You can move forward with confidence since His ability will equip you to accomplish any task that He places before you. The time is now to pursue all that the Lord has for you.

1. Phillip R. Johnson, "The Obedience of Faith," *The Spurgeon Archive* [online], 2001 [cited 26 January 2010]. Available from the Internet: *www.spurgeon.org/sermons/2195.html.*

ABUNDANT

God's New People

In effect Paul told his Jewish readers that God has created a third race, a new society of people called the body of Christ (Eph. 3:1-19). This new group isn't exclusively Jew or Gentile but includes people from all groups (v. 6). He explained to the Jewish believers at Ephesus that Christ's blood shed on Calvary for the remission of their sins wasn't just for them. That blood was also for the Gentiles, those who are not Jewish. Aren't we glad for that?

Paul was outlining for them a great mystery, this third race, this new society, and saying that the body of Christ was to include both Jew and Gentile. You need to understand how foreign this concept would've been. It's kind of like in our country, 50, 60, or 70 years ago. If someone believed that there would ever be a time when black people and white people and Asian people and Hispanic people would all be in the same place worshiping the one true God at the same time, they would have been laughed at.

In what way was Paul's address to the body of Christ at Ephesus ahead of its time in regard to social and racial desegregation?

If the body of Christ is a third race, how well are we demonstrating this in America at our current collective bodies?

What do you believe most hinders our churches from becoming a fully blended third race?

In what ways does Paul's remark to the church at Ephesus rebuke any form of racism within the body of Christ?

What does it mean to be a member of this new society?

Not only are we called to release our allegiance to our genetic race when by faith we come into the body of Christ, but we also are reminded that everything else about us is changed.

How could you use 2 Corinthians 5:17 to encourage new believers of all races to join together in their worship of the Lord?

This third race is composed of individuals not physically born into it but rather who enter through a common personal faith in Jesus Christ. This common faith is so extreme and yet personal that all members share in its blessing regardless of biological gender, race, or economic status.

Use Galatians 3:28 to describe how salvation and a relationship with Christ is not dependent on one's age, race, or economic status.

In what ways do you see this verse fulfilled in your church?

In what ways do you need to pray for this verse to be fulfilled in your church in the future?

Even our identities as citizens are challenged when we become members of the body of Christ. Faith in Christ not only eradicates boundaries between races but also the hedges of nationalities. God does not want us placing our primary hope or identity in anything other than our personal relationship with Him.

How does Acts 10:34-35 demonstrate that God is neither impressed by our individual nationalities nor shows favoritism to any particular one?

What warning do you find in those verses for people who may assume that just because they live in a Christian nation God will show favor on them?

Use Philippians 3:20 to describe a healthy understanding of citizenship for those in this third race.

How does your life demonstrate citizenship in heaven?

In Ephesians 2 Paul wrote about the foundation for unity found in Christ for those who are part of the third race. Read Ephesians 2:11-22 and answer the following questions:

What was Paul challenging the believers to remember (vv. 11-13)?

Why must we never forget that we were once separated from the body of Christ?

How ought a common faith in Christ put to death any hostility between races?

Years ago I wrote in my journal a desire that I believe God put in my heart—for Going Beyond Ministries to be used as a bridge between races and denominations. Our prayer is that in some small way we might contribute to the mending of divisions within the body. Conclude today's lesson by considering how God might use you and your church to assist in this effort.

Mission Impossible

Paul wrote the Christians not only to point to their own impossible situation but also while he was in the middle of his own. The Book of Ephesians is called a Prison Epistle because Paul wrote these letters from a Roman prison. He was probably under house arrest for two years, a circumstance nobody would like to be in.

There Paul sat, disappointed, probably frustrated, ready to be done with this particular season of life. He was in an impossible personal situation, and yet right in the middle of that impossibility, he encouraged other believers by saying in essence, "Now is the time, despite life's difficulty, to consider the ability, the greatness, the grandeur of my God." In this Prison Epistle, Ephesians 3:20-21 is a doxology. A doxology is an outpouring of praise and worship and honor to God.

What impossible situation do you currently face?

Does your reaction tend to be more a dirge or a doxology?

Have you ever had to worship God despite a prison-like setting?
If so, please share.

Right in the middle of personal impossible situations, Paul emphasized the "nowness" of worshiping God. Not another time or another place. Right now is the time for you to believe and experience the abundance, the greatness, the fullness that your God has come to give even in the face of frustration.

Describe your typical reaction to God during what seemed to be an impossible situation.

How has God used those times in your past to draw you into a closer relationship with Him?

Why do you think some people find it easier to worship God during the difficult times than during the easy times?

John 10:10 is one of my favorite passages. You know it well. It says the enemy has come to kill, to steal, and to destroy. To kill, steal, and destroy what? The promise of what Jesus said He had come to give. "I have come that they might have life, and that they might have it more abundantly." That is to the full and overflowing. That's the kind of life that He had come to give.

How have you experienced the abundant, full, and overflowing life offered by Christ?

In what ways has Satan attempted to kill, steal, or destroy the divine abundance Jesus has offered you?

How can you use those times of experiencing God's abundant blessings to endure the times Satan attempts to attack you?

As I've considered different seasons of my life, it's occurred to me that I've often been waiting on my circumstances to change before feeling like I can experience God's abundance. We often think: *If I can just get out of this season and into the next one, then I know abundance will be waiting for me. If I can just get out of this disappointing, frustrating circumstance I'm in, then I know I'll experience God's best.*

Have you ever simply endured a season of life, hoping that in the next phase you would receive the abundant life promised by Christ? If so, when?

How were your desires met or unmet upon the arrival of the next season?

The apostle Paul desired to rearrange our thinking on that. The abundant life is not when no impossible situations occur and you're experiencing peace, joy, and happiness. While that's nice, true abundance is really seen when you're sitting in a prison circumstance, when you're eye to eye with an impossible situation, and right in the heart of your impossible, you experience the fullness of God. When, like Paul, we can pour out our honor and praise upon God and maybe even write a doxology of our own in spite of what we're going through—that, my friend, is the abundant life.

Using 2 Corinthians 12:9, please answer the following questions:

According to this verse, how do we miss out on the blessings of God's abundant provision when we simply endure seasons rather than seek Him in the midst of hardships?

What correlation did Paul give between our weakness and our ability to display God's power in our lives?

How does this verse challenge you in your ability to boast during times of hardship or suffering?

While in prison, Paul prayed specifically for the body of Christ in Ephesus that they would have spiritual strength. He was a prisoner himself, and yet he prayed that they would have strength. Paul was intimately acquainted with suffering. Read Ephesians 3:14-21 and consider the specific requests Paul made on behalf of his brothers and sisters during their times of hardship.

In this prayer, what role does the Holy Spirit play in bringing encouragement to believers?

What was the role of faith in this prayer?

How does this prayer demonstrate the importance of unity and love among the believers during times of hardship?

According to verses 20-21, what confidence did Paul have in Christ's desire and ability to comfort and strengthen those who were enduring hardship?

Only a person being comforted by God's Spirit can extend worship to Him in spite of difficult situations. As you end today's lesson, write a doxology to God. Then read it aloud to Him in prayer.

Time for a Turning

Miss Kay reminded us from Hebrews that we must fix our eyes on Jesus who is the author and the perfecter of our faith. Fix your eyes on Jesus. Turn your attention to Him. There's only one way to do that. Pivot your attention away from that which is bugging you, away from the frustration, away from the seemingly impossible. Turn your attention away from that which so often pulls your attention toward it. Deliberately, consciously turn your attention away. Pivot 180 degrees until your attention is focused on Jesus Christ.

What situations in your life right now claim your constant attention?

In what sense are these situations drawing you closer to Christ?

In what sense are they pulling you further away from your relationship with Christ?

Hebrews 12:2 begins by saying, "Let us fix our eyes on Jesus." This word "fix" means to intentionally set our gaze upon Him with purpose. If our eyes are "fixed" on something, they are watching with intent.

Have your eyes ever been fixed on Christ? What did this look like in your life?

How did fixing your eyes on Christ affect your attitude during times that sought to distract you from Him?

What role do personal Bible study and prayer play in our ability to purposely set our gaze on Christ?

Scripture clearly states that we will constantly be changing between seasons of life. Each season will bring with it a unique set of blessings as well as distractions. The key for us to healthily maneuver through each is two-part: First, realize that they are but for a moment, and second, fix our gaze on Christ.

The Book of Ecclesiastes reminds us that seasons of life will come and go. Despite how we feel about life situations, each is only temporary. If we fix our gaze on the seasons rather than on Christ, we can become overwhelmed. Remembering to hold fast to Christ, however, will enable us to walk faithfully.

Starting with verse 2, write one way you can find peace during a particular season by setting your gaze on Christ:

[1]There is a time for everything,
    and a season for every activity under heaven:

[2]a time to be born and a time to die,
    a time to plant and a time to uproot,

[3]a time to kill and a time to heal,
    a time to tear down and a time to build,

[4]a time to weep and a time to laugh,
    a time to mourn and a time to dance,

[5]a time to scatter stones and a time to gather them,
    a time to embrace and a time to refrain,

[6]a time to search and a time to give up,
    a time to keep and a time to throw away,

[7]a time to tear and a time to mend,
    a time to be silent and a time to speak,

[8]a time to love and a time to hate,
    a time for war and a time for peace.

Our peace is also derived from the understanding that although we are in a perpetual set of changing life seasons, Christ is constant. He does not change. He is the same today as He was yesterday.

How can Christ's constancy despite our seasons of change bring you peace in any situation?

In light of this, how would you best explain the foolishness of our setting our gaze on other people or situations instead of Christ?

What is the relationship between our personal stability despite our current season of life and the object our eyes are fixed upon?

Since Christ is constant, we must abide in Him. After we turn our gaze toward Christ, we must next abide in Him.

Read John 15:4-8 and answer the following questions:

What is the promise of Christ's faithfulness found in verse 4?

Have you sought to produce fruit without remaining in Him during difficult seasons? If so, how; and how did it work?

How do verses 5-8 explain God's desire for us to turn toward Christ at all times and during all seasons?

Keeping your sights fixed will not be easy when so many other interests and concerns compete for your attention. Doing this will require a deliberate, daily choice. But don't think for a moment that it is a task you can't handle. God's Spirit will empower you to keep your eyes right where they belong.

the
other
side of
darkness

{ Brigitte Kitenge had a promising life: a loving husband with a good job, beautiful daughters, and the opportunity to advance her education. But on April 6, 1994, everything changed.

by Dawn Hollomon

Photography by Joseph Anthony Baker

THE NIGHTMARE BEGAN for Leon and Brigitte Kitenge one April evening in 1994 when the lights went out in Rwanda's capital city of Kigali. Leon, a Congolese man, had a good job as a marketing director. His wife, Brigitte, a Tutsi woman, was studying international law at a university. They thought the power outage was a momentary glitch in their promising lives. In reality, it was the beginning of a long and painful journey through darkness. The next morning Brigitte's sister called to tell them that the president had been assassinated (see sidebar "Rwanda 1994"). She urged Leon to take Brigitte and their two daughters to the Democratic Republic of the Congo (Congo) for safety. It was the last time the Kitenges would ever hear from her.

Brigitte endured tortures of which she would never be able to speak.

The night the president was killed, extremist Hutus, the majority tribe in Rwanda, began killing the minority Tutsis. Fearing for her life, Brigitte hid in a hole in the ground for 10 days. She emerged only at night to nurse their 3-month-old daughter, Axelle.

Leon had to tell Arlette, who was 4 years old, that Brigitte was dead so she wouldn't give away her mom's whereabouts. When Hutus came to look for Brigitte and couldn't find her, they beat Leon so badly that he bled in his ears.

"I could see the fear of death in his eyes," Brigitte recalls. "I had to make a very serious decision. I knew that if we stayed, Leon and my children would be killed. If we left, I would be killed."

> "I could see the fear of death in his eyes. If we stayed, he and my children would be killed. If we left, I would be killed."
> —Brigitte Kitenge

The family made a break for the Congolese embassy. At one checkpoint, Leon was forced to give their car for ransom so Brigitte would not be hurt. The couple was forced to flee on foot with a toddler and a baby. They hid during the day and ran at night.

"Bodies were piling up like wood," Brigitte recalls. "I had questions without answers for God."

Leon carried Arlette on his back, and Brigitte, weak from trauma, found the strength to carry baby Axelle. Eventually, Leon was able to secure seats on a bus headed for Congo. However, the rest of the mostly Hutu passengers were angry that the bus driver had allowed a Tutsi to ride. But the Hutu bus driver refused to allow Brigitte to be killed on his bus.

No Tutsis had survived past the last checkpoint before Congo. "Nobody of my kind escaped this place," Brigitte explains. Hutus pulled Brigitte and Arlette aside. While waiting in line to be killed, Arlette asked Brigitte, "'Mommy, why are these people sleeping in blood? Tell them to wake up!'" Brigitte recalls. "She didn't understand. I covered her face."

Brigitte ran back to Leon to say goodbye: "Thank you for being a good husband. Thank you for loving me." When Brigitte said these things, Leon began screaming.

"I thought of her dreams and a future that she had hoped for, her young age," Leon says. "There I was, standing waiting to see my wife killed, unable to protect her. I was powerless."

Then he showed a Hutu official his wedding certificate. Because Brigitte and Leon had been married prior to the crisis, the official spared her and allowed her to proceed to Congo.

Living in Congo with Leon's relatives wasn't the refuge that Brigitte needed. His family disapproved of their marriage because he had married outside of his tribe. But their life calmed down enough for Brigitte to complete her degree in business management.

Brigitte was working for an American humanitarian organization. But when political tensions escalated, Brigitte was accused of being a spy and was thrown in and out of jail because of her association with Americans. "I was like a leaf from a tree. I didn't know where I would fall. I didn't know where I would end," Brigitte explains.

Brigitte's last time in jail was particularly difficult. Tortures happened to her there of which she would never be able to speak. "The last time they released me, I told myself, *I cannot go through this. It can't happen to me anymore,*"

Rwanda 1994

When Rwanda was colonized in the 18th century, the colonizers elevated the minority Tutsi tribe over the majority Hutu. In 1958, a wave of independence spread across many African countries, including Rwanda, Burundi, and Congo. Many Tutsis were driven out of Rwanda. In 1990, many Tutsis began asking to return, but the president, a Hutu, wouldn't allow it. North of Rwanda, along the Ugandan border, Tutsis began fighting their way back into the country. In 1993, the Hutu and the Tutsis agreed to a cease-fire, but the president didn't want to sign. Strong international opinion, however, forced the president's hand.

In 1994, the Rwandan president and the president of Burundi had gone to Tanzania to sign the document to allow the Tutsis to return. On April 6, the plane carrying both presidents was shot down. To this day, responsibility for the assassinations is unknown. It was on this night that Hutus began killing Tutsis. From April 6 to mid-July of 1994, nearly one million Rwandans were killed.

Throughout their long journey,
Leon fought to save
Brigitte's life time
and time again.

she recalls. "I took my Bible and I said to God, 'If You are really God, in a few minutes I am going to face [You] and ask You questions.'" Then, to commit suicide, Brigitte threw herself into Lake Kivu, where the bodies of many genocide victims still floated. But Brigitte was rescued and taken to a hospital, where she remained in a coma for many days. When she awoke, angry at herself and angry at God that she hadn't died, she learned that she was pregnant with their third daughter, Anita.

In July 1998, the situation in Congo worsened, and Brigitte and her family fled to Uganda. Once again, the Kitenge family was on the run.

Desperate for a sign that God did exist, Brigitte sneaked into a church. The pastor singled her out and told her that God was going to lift her up and people would know that only God had done it.

Brigitte didn't believe what he said, but the prophecy began a work in her heart. Although she was still hurting, Leon and Brigitte began a house church called Restoration Fellowship. "I was wounded inside, full of hatred, but I wanted to help other people," Brigitte explains.

Another pastor visited the fellowship and prayed a blessing over her: "'God is going to fill you with love. The enemy has stolen your heart; he has abused you; he has killed you. Now the Lord is going to restore you because He is going to use you to restore other people.'" The pastor rebuked hatred and asked God to fill her with His love. The blessing was powerful.

"I began loving people," Brigitte says. "Even now people are suspicious because I love them so much. I can't survive now without people."

Brigitte began pleading with United Nations officials to gain refugee status so her family could leave the country. They hoped to go to a country where they could use the French language skills they learned in school. Eventually, Brigitte connected with a woman who was offering legal aid to refugees to help them gain asylum in the United States. The Kitenges arrived in Nashville, Tenn., on September 25, 2000. A local church helped the family begin their new life. But with all the differences in lifestyle, language, and culture, the family went into deep shock.

"I was exhausted emotionally and physically from all these years of running and hiding," Brigitte explains. "I needed time to scream, cry, and empty my heart, but I had to be strong for my family."

Leon, who had previously worked in professional settings, was given a manual labor job working in construction. For a slight African man, working outside in the winter with heavy jackhammers was difficult.

The daughters also struggled with the transition. They had missed entire grades of school. Kids from school would sometimes call them names.

As Brigitte watched her family struggle, she knew she needed to make a change. She and Leon began to see themselves as missionaries, not refugees. "When I was brought to America as a refugee, I came with many unanswered questions, but I wasn't ready to let go as if nothing had happened

"When I see the scars on my body, I see the work of the evil one, but moreover I see grace springing through each of my scars."
—Brigitte Kitenge

in my life. I wanted answers; I wanted change. Deep inside I knew that in order to see the change, I must change the way I see my past, my journey, and everything in between."

Brigitte began sharing her testimony at churches. She worked on her English and began attending seminary classes. She knew God had brought her to the United States for a purpose. She later received a master's and a doctoral degree from seminary.

In 2001, God gave Leon and Brigitte a vision to be a voice for the people of Africa. "God has always called two people for His work," Leon explains. "As for His disciples. Jesus called them in teams of two by two. I believe that Brigitte and I are called to serve the Lord together." The couple founded African Global Mission to help train African pastors who have little education or formal training to do the work of God (see sidebar "A Heart for Africa").

Now the Kitenges are helping the same people who caused them so much pain for many years. "In Rwanda the women I serve are all survivors of the genocide of 1994, and in Congo I am serving women who are living in hopelessness and violence. I identify with these women. Knowing the pain and despair of not being able to feed their children, I am moved with compassion toward them," Brigitte explains.

"I innocently became a victim; many of these women are victims as well. I see these women as fellow sisters, and I am committed to help them. Hutu or Tutsi, it doesn't bother me anymore. I have seen the love of the Lord that surpasses all understanding," Brigitte says.

"I am a woman who has suffered so much, but I also have seen God's goodness and deliverance. I have seen the mighty hand of God protecting me and guiding me through it all. I have been rescued and restored by the love of God; therefore, I have forgiven my torturers, those who killed my family members. My prayer is that wherever they are, they will discover the goodness of God and become aware of His unlimited love. I pray that the goodness of God will lead them to repentance," Brigitte confesses.

"When by the grace of God I became aware of the love of God for me in the midst of those hard moments, I made a choice to make peace with my past. I closed the door to hatred and moved to a place called forgiveness. And love healed me. Today I can look back and see the unseen hand of God uncovering my stinky wounds and bandaging them with love and forgiveness."

In May of this year, Brigitte made her first trip back to Rwanda, 14 years after she left. She didn't know how much strength she would need to see the ruins of her old house and the ruins of her families' houses. But it helped her heart to see how far her home country has come.

"I wish I could say that I held on to God through these nightmares. But the truth is that God held me tightly. I am not proud of what I went through, but I am proud of what God is doing with what I went through to strengthen many lives."

Brigitte says her scars from years of pain and violence serve as reminders of where God has brought her family today. "When I see the scars on my body, I see the work of the evil one, but moreover I see grace springing through each of my scars. Instead of cursing and grieving as I used to do, I bless my torturers and praise God for His deliverance, restoration, and grace. Today I can tell anyone who is going through injustice, abuse, and rejection that there is no deep pit that the hand of God can't reach. He is mighty to save." □

The Kitenges are a vibrant, loving family:
(back row) Arlette, Axelle, Leon, Anita
(front row) Brigitte, Arrielle

A Heart for Africa

AFRICAN GLOBAL MISSION was founded to train African church leaders and ministry workers. Bible schools are few and far between, and many are far away enough to require pastors to move their families and leave their churches behind for two years. Understandably, many pastors aren't willing to abandon their churches. The ministry of African Global Mission has since expanded to include:

▶ Training Leaders: training local pastors where they are and equipping them to shepherd their congregations.
▶ Youth on Mission: seeking to raise a new generation of Africans to be leaders.
▶ Future Hope for Women: giving African women who are struggling to recover from war and violence hope and job skills so they can earn income for their families.

Learn more about these ministries and how you can help at *africanglobalmission.org*.

As We Forgive

AN AMAZING WORK of reconciliation is happening today in Rwanda. Where the church failed its people in 1994, it is now working to rebuild a unified Rwanda. As *We Forgive*, directed by Laura Waters Hinson, is a stunning documentary about how Rwandans are helping other Rwandans to forgive and move forward. Find out more at *asweforgive.com*.

VIEWERGUIDE

SEVEN PRINCIPLES IN EPHESIANS 3:20-21

1. Time

2. Turning

3. _____

      John 2:11

      Micah 7:7

      You either _____ God or you don't.

      Jeremiah 29:11

4. _____

      Paul uses the word *hyper* twice in Ephesians 3:20.

      We serve a God who does _____ past your way past.

5. _____

       Every single thing that concerns you _____ _____.

       Matthew 10:30

       Romans 8:32

       We have a God who _____ about _____.

6. _____ power

7. Our _____ to Him

       Our God is _____ in His character, but He is

       _____ in His activity.

GROUP DISCUSSION QUESTIONS

1. God is predictable in His character, but He is unpredictable in His activity. In what ways has God been predictable in your life?

2. In what ways has God's unpredictable activity surprised you?

WEEK FOUR | DAY ONE
Dynamite Power

I'm so excited about the rich treasure available to unearth in the words and phrases we will consider this week. One of my favorites in all of Scripture is up next. The Holy Spirit's *dunamis* is an explosive power that can completely change and alter the structure of a thing.

Are you in a relationship that needs to be restructured? God can do it. Do you have a heart that needs to be rearranged? God can do it. Has a financial debacle taken you by storm in this fragile economy? Lean in and listen carefully, my friend. We serve a God who's able. He's got explosive power that can do beyond your wildest dreams. Dynamite power.

What would you say has been the greatest display of the Holy Spirit's power you've seen in your life?

How has He shown His power in the life of someone you know?

Why do you suppose we forget so quickly how able our God is? List reasons and plan to talk about this with your group this week.

The power God has by virtue of inherent ability and resources—why is this important? Because Paul was teaching us that the power God has is actually a part of who He is. Our God does not *have* power; He *is* the powerful One. That means if you see God doing something miraculous for somebody else, you don't have to stand back and wonder whether or not He might have enough power left for you. Since God is His own source of power, He is not dependent on anyone or anything else.

If we understand that God is eternal and His source of power is innate within Himself, how does that change how we see His ability to meet needs?

How can you find rest and solace in recognizing the limitless power of the Holy Spirit?

When God disperses power, He is no less powerful than He was before He gave that power away. God is completely full of power and can never exhaust His resources. Our God is all-powerful and He is all-powerful all of the time. You cannot out-ask, out-request, or out-pray the ability of God. Your wildest imagination cannot out-dream His ability in your life.

Have you ever avoided making requests to God? If so, what were the requests, and why did you not make them?

What does our reluctance to ask the Holy Spirit to help us accomplish things beyond our wildest imagination say about our faith in His ability?

List two specific ways that your life would be different if you were able to place full faith and confidence in God's power to accomplish anything you need or desire.

For the rest of today's lesson I want you to consider what I call "turbo" power that's supposed to be working on the inside of us. The Scriptures describe an energy, an engine-like power that's supposed to be operating in us daily. Ephesians 1:13-14 says the moment you believe, you receive the Holy Spirit of God. The Holy Spirit is God Himself. The fullness, the greatness, the grandeur, the authority that is inherent in God the Father is also inherent in the Holy Spirit. That means if the Holy Spirit lives in you, the ability and the power of God the Father is also inside of you.

Do you feel it is apparent to others that you are indwelt with the turbo power of the Holy Spirit? If so, list some specific reasons.

In what ways have you lived your life as though the only strength available to you was your own?

Beyond power, what amazing promise of hope and assurance does the Holy Spirit bring (Eph. 1:13-14)?

When speaking to His disciples, Jesus took time to inform them that God's power would soon come to earth in the Holy Spirit (John 16). In verses 12-14, He promised the Holy Spirit would guide them into all truth. Numerous blessings found in the Holy Spirit are ours for the taking.

Each of the following verses share important information about the role and function of the Holy Spirit. Read each verse and describe in your own words what it teaches you.

Luke 12:11-12

John 14:6

John 16:13-14

Acts 1:8

2 Timothy 1:13-14

According to 1 Corinthians 2:6-12, what is the relationship between being indwelt by the power of the Holy Spirit and our ability to understand Scripture and the ways of God?

When you think about it, God has already given us the most astounding gift we could ever be given. The Holy Spirit was the most generous present that the Father could offer. And He did, the moment we were saved. So make it your priority to cherish and become fully acquainted with this most precious gift in your everyday living.

Unbelieving Disciples

As I mentioned, I've been in the church as long as I can remember. I have been sitting on the pews of a church hearing the Word of God taught with power. I won Sword drills, sang all the hymns, and clamored to be the first to answer my Sunday School teachers' questions. I'm certain that I was a bit annoying.

I knew all the stuff I should, but I have spent most of my Christian life not really believing that all I knew was true for me. What a tragedy it was to have Him living within me, know Scripture, and be acquainted with the ability of God but not recognize the connection between my reality and His ability. I realized I wasn't even praying about some things because I was afraid to put that on God's plate. I was fearful that my needs might be minor compared with others' concerns and if He didn't move as I was requesting, that might disappoint me too much. He's got other stuff to do, you know? He doesn't have time for my little ole thing.

Can you personally relate to Priscilla's testimony? If so, how?

How is it possible to know all the right things and know all the right answers and yet still not really believe it is relevant for you?

Why would it be a tragedy for a believer to know many things about God yet doubt the promises are true for her as an individual?

Do you believe some aspects of God's character or blessings are true, yet you have never asked for them to be made real in your life? If so, what are they?

What has kept you from asking for them so far?

I was spiritually asleep. The Lord used John 2 to shake me awake. The passage tells the miracle of Jesus turning water into wine. His disciples were there. They saw the whole thing, and John 2:11 tells us their reaction to what they saw. It says, "The disciples believed in Him" (NASB). Hear that again:

The disciples believed—only after they saw this miracle.

That tells us it is possible to be a disciple and still not believe God.

My friend, a person can walk with God, talk with Him, pray to Him, serve Him and be in church sitting on the pew learning about Him, but not trust God with her life. A woman can fail to believe what He can do for her even when she's heard and maybe even seen what God can do for other people. She can learn about God but not really believe it's all true for her.

How would you describe the difference between belief and trust?

Do you identify in any way with the disciples—learning about God yet not fully believing? Explain.

Have you ever experienced a "water turning into wine" moment when God's power was made very evident in the life of someone else? Please describe the circumstance.

How did this experience encourage your own faith in Him?

What danger do you see in believing God only when we experience one of those "water turning into wine" moments?

Why do you suppose we think we will believe God when we witness His power at work in someone's life rather than simply believing Him in faith through the promises of Scripture?

Jesus Christ realized the difficulty of faith. Although we are instructed in Hebrews that without faith it is impossible to please God, we are never told that having faith is easy. When preparing for His impending departure, Christ encouraged His disciples in their current faith, and He also went beyond the present to encourage all of us who would follow in their footsteps.

What does John 20:29 say to you about the need to always have visible or tangible evidence before we place faith in God's promises?

Rather than waiting for evidence to believe God's promises, our faith should precede the evidence. Micah 7:7 says, "But as for me, I watch in hope for the LORD, I wait for God my Savior; my God will hear me." We see Micah's confidence in God's ability to answer him in his final statement, "My God will hear me."

How are you currently "watching" for God to supply a need?

How are you currently "waiting" for God to answer a prayer?

How are your actions or attitude confirming that you believe "my God will hear me"?

When we focus our attention on the character and promises of God, our faith much more easily precedes the need for evidence. Read and rejoice in Zephaniah 3:17 as you end today's study.

Our Unmanageable God

We must always remember that God's beyond, His way past, is so beyond our wildest imagination that it doesn't necessarily mean it's a matter of making us happy right here and now. His kingdom purposes are so beyond. They are so grand and are being worked out in such a way that they might be beyond our mental capacity to comprehend. We cannot view it all and see the effects of God's purposes from one generation to the next. That can be frustrating when we want the miracle we want. We desire a tangible answer in our situation right now, but God's plans are so way past our way past that even in the Book of John, He told the disciples, in essence, *Some things I cannot even tell you because they would be too much for you to handle.* ("I have much more to say to you, more than you can now bear," John 16:12.)

Have you ever asked God for a tangible answer and He made you wait to receive it?

How did you respond to His delayed answer?

Were there results that might not have happened without the delay?

Why do you think we often become so frustrated with the Lord when we perceive that answers to our prayers are being delayed?

After reading the following verses, describe how misapplication could result in great frustration for a believer whose desires remain unmet.

"If you believe, you will receive whatever you ask for in prayer" (Matt. 21:22).

"Therefore I tell you, whatever you ask for in prayer, believe that you have received it, and it will be yours" (Mark 11:24).

"Even now God will give you whatever you ask" (John 11:22).

"I will do whatever you ask in my name, so that the Son may bring glory to the Father" (John 14:13).

"You did not choose me, but I chose you and appointed you to go and bear fruit—fruit that will last. Then the Father will give you whatever you ask in my name" (John 15:16).

"In that day you will no longer ask me anything. I tell you the truth, my Father will give you whatever you ask in my name" (John 16:23).

How could a misapplication of these verses cause confusion?

How would you explain to a new believer the idea that God doesn't always cater to our wants?

Jesus encountered such a situation with His close friends, Mary and Martha. Upon discovering the extreme illness of their brother, Lazarus, they sent immediately for help from Jesus. They wanted their need met NOW! Yet, because His ways are beyond our own, Jesus delayed in responding.

Use the story of Lazarus, John 11:1-46, to answer the following:

What promise and purpose does verse 4 give for the illness attacking Lazarus?

Would this response encourage or frustrate you? How so?

According to verse 6, how long did Christ wait before He began to respond to the news?

What was Martha's view of Christ and His relationship to God the Father (vv. 21-22)?

How did Mary and Martha differ in their responses to Christ?

According to verses 45 and 46, what do you believe was Christ's kingdom purpose in delaying His response to Mary and Martha?

How do you maintain the balance of a truly robust faith with the fact that God has not relinquished His sovereignty to you or anybody else?

The same God who said "whatever you ask" also warned:

"All this I have told you so that you will not go astray" (John 16:1).

"They will put you out of the synagogue; in fact, a time is coming when anyone who kills you will think he is offering a service to God" (John 16:2).

"I tell you the truth, you will weep and mourn while the world rejoices. You will grieve, but your grief will turn to joy" (John 16:20).

"A woman giving birth to a child has pain because her time has come; but when her baby is born she forgets the anguish because of her joy that a child is born into the world" (John 16:21).

"So with you: Now is your time of grief, but I will see you again and you will rejoice, and no one will take away your joy" (John 16:22).

"I have told you these things, so that in me you may have peace. In this world you will have trouble. But take heart! I have overcome the world" (John 16:33).

Use the preceding verses to contrast the relationship between God's ability to exceedingly meet your needs with the warning that life will have times of grief and sorrow.

How could you use those verses to encourage a believer with a desperate prayer request that has long remained unanswered?

God made sunsets and sunrises. He exceeds all expectations. When you know your God is transcendent, that His ability and His truth go infinitely beyond you, then it causes you to pray differently. When you know who you're dealing with, it changes how you relate to Him. It makes you believe for bigger things. You expect more fully than you ever expected because you know that the God you're talking to is not just able (transcendentally—beyond the beyond), but He also loves you and has your best interests in mind.

How have you experienced God going beyond to give you small glimpses of eternity?

In what way does your faith that God always has your best interest in mind help you remain encouraged even when you're waiting to see Him respond to a need?

I've gotta tell you, I've been asking the Lord about some things for years now. While I'm tempted to be discouraged as time continues to pass, I'm encouraged when I consider what we've contemplated today. God cares for us and is, right now, factoring in divine purposes and plans in relation to our requests. Let's keep trusting and keep pressing in to Him. Today and every day.

Praying Expectantly

We took a trip to New York with my family, my parents, all three of my siblings, our spouses, and our kids. One evening at dinner I noticed that my sister's husband, Jessie, was ordering a little appetizer as his entrée for the second night in a row. Now, some men in some other families might eat lightly, but the guys in my family are big, football-player types who think that anything less than meat and potatoes should be labeled "rabbit food." They don't eat appetizers unless it's just a preface to the real deal.

So I leaned over to him and asked, "Are you not feeling well?"

He responded, "No, I'm feeling fine, but I've got a large family with lots of mouths to feed. This restaurant is kind of expensive, so I'm just eating an appetizer and then I'll go out on the street and get a hot dog from one of the street vendors."

I looked at him in bewilderment and asked if he'd gotten the memo that our parents had sent via e-mail several days before our trip. It had clearly said that they'd cover the bill for dinner each night.

He almost choked on a bite of his tiny hors d'oeuvre. "What? I have been hungry for two days!" He called the waitress over and ordered the biggest steak he could get. It seems that knowing someone with adequate resources had him covered changed his perception of what his options really were.

Knowing God and the resources He's made available to you will change the way you order, my friend. It changes not only how you pray but what you feel free to ask God for. You will begin to realize that you don't have to pray small or with reservation. You can ask the Lord for exactly what you desire no matter how outlandish or impossible it may appear to be. Your Father has got you covered, so look at the menu differently.

Have you ever gone hungry in some area of your life because you didn't believe that God could exceedingly and abundantly meet your needs? How so?

Is there anything that keeps you from praying expectantly to God?

How would your prayer life change if you fully embraced the truth that God "can cover this one"?

As I've begun to recognize the great resources at God's disposal, my prayer life sure has changed. While I still present my desires to Him, I conclude prayers with this statement: "God, do this or something better." While my request might have been good, I want to always leave room for God to do beyond my expectations.

What fears might someone have about concluding her prayers with a statement like Priscilla's?

If someone were to evaluate your prayer life, would she find you to be one who always plays it safe or one who prays expectantly for things beyond her control? What evidence would she see?

The Gospel of Matthew is a wonderful example of how we should pray. Matthew 6 encourages us not to get caught up in how we look or sound praying but instead to simply go to God privately and pour out our hearts to Him. We do not have to use lofty sentences or words beyond our understanding for God to hear us. Verse 8 reminds us that God already knows what you need before you ask Him.

Use the Lord's Prayer in Matthew 6:9-13 as an outline to write a personal prayer of expectancy to God.

"Our Father in heaven, hallowed be your name,

your kingdom come, your will be done on earth as it is in heaven.

Give us today our daily bread.

Forgive us our debts, as we also have forgiven our debtors.

And lead us not into temptation, but deliver us from the evil one."

Matthew 7 goes on to remind us that God desires to give you good things. When we pray without great expectation, we are either implying that God is unable to fully answer our prayers or that He would not desire to do so.

In what ways does Matthew 7:9-11 encourage you to pray more boldly?

Absolutely nothing is wrong with you having a box into which you file away what you're learning about God and what He has done in your life. The problem comes when we put a lid on it. What nerve we must have to ever think we can close God in the confines of our little container and assume that if He wants to do anything outside of it, then it must not be God.

Listen to me. Our God is predictable in His character, but He is unpredictable in His activity. You cannot box God in. When you put your lid on a box, it doesn't limit God; it limits your awareness of God. He's still moving and speaking, yet you can be unaware of His transcendence, His greatness, and His ability because it's outside of your little box.

Does your prayer life reflect that you have put a lid on your box? If so, how?

What caused you to shut the lid in the first place?

Do you have a spiritual box with a closed lid that has been limiting your view of God's movement in your life? If you've stopped praying about something particular because you really don't think He'll do anything substantial, then you can be sure your lid is airtight. Whether God moves is a question of His sovereignty, not His ability. What He does is His business. Believing that He *can* is our business.

Have you stopped praying about something because the lid of your box is shut?

Describe your plans to reopen the lid to your box for God.

Write a prayer of expectancy to end our time together today. I'm asking our God to give you a robust faith that will be bold enough to take off lids and put on an eagerness and anticipation for the great things He has in store.

God of the Little Stuff

All. A simple but powerful word. I researched it in the original language and after all that investigating, *all* just means *all.* It's a good thing since we've got plenty of concerns, huh?

Every single thing that concerns you concerns God. That's right; all of it. Every little detail of your life is on the mind of God. All this talk about the grandeur and greatness of God may tempt you to think the little things in your life might not cross His mind. But you can rest assured that He cares about it *all,* not just if it's big but also if it's small.

If you were to honestly bring all things before God in prayer, how would your prayer life differ?

What details of your life have you neglected to bring before God in prayer because you have assumed that they are too small?

If we are really aware that God is concerned about the mundane things, why don't we consistently bring them to Him in prayer?

How do we make the distinction between the big things we bring to God and the small things we often fail to bring to Him in prayer?

Our attitude and ability to find peace in the midst of situations may often be directly tied to our understanding of prayer. Philippians 4:6 states, "Do not be anxious about anything, but in everything, by prayer and petition, with thanksgiving, present your requests to God." We can needlessly suffer anxiety due to our unwillingness to hand over our requests and petitions to God.

What little things in your life cause you to become anxious?

Have you needlessly suffered anxiety over an issue due to a reluctance to bring it before God in prayer?

What does it mean to be thankful for things we are in prayer over?

How do you give thanks if your prayer request is something that causes you pain or anxiety?

In what way does sharing our small things with God in prayer help nurture a more intimate relationship with Him?

Romans 8:32 asks, Since God delivered His Son up for us all, "how will He not also with Him freely give us all things?" (NASB). In other words, "If I loved you enough to die for you, don't you think I love you enough to take care of you? Don't you think that the little things that concern you are things that indeed concern me?" And honestly, there really are no small concerns, are there? Because if it's something that's bothering you, it is not small, is it? It certainly doesn't feel that way. If it's important to you, then rest assured that it's important to God.

Where does the scale for big things and small things come from? Since as humans we typically delight in doing small things for those we love, why do you think we often find it so difficult to believe that God would also delight in meeting our needs?

In what way can the thought *this issue is too small to pray about* be a lie from Satan?

What role do you think personal arrogance plays in our decision to say some things are too small to pray about?

God has great appreciation for what we may consider the small details of life. Matthew 10:29-31 says, "Are not two sparrows sold for a penny? Yet not one of them will fall to the ground apart from the will of your Father. And even the very hairs of your head are all numbered. So don't be afraid; you are worth more than many sparrows."

Jesus pointed out how little earthly value is placed on sparrows. Yet despite their earthly value, the Father is keenly aware of their activity. Isn't it comforting that our God is not just equated with generalities but is also concerned with our specifics as well?

List some things that carry little earthy value yet are of great importance to you.

If we as humans can care for and appreciate things that seem of little worth, why do we often find it so difficult to understand that God is concerned about the small things in our lives?

How does the fact that God is in full control over things that we as humans may consider mundane affect our understanding of how God views our supposedly mundane request?

It's been a pleasure to study with you over these two weeks. I know that Miss Beth has more for you that you'll not want to miss. But before you move on, take time to contemplate what you've considered the last two weeks. Write down the main principles that the Lord spoke to your heart and how your life will be affected and changed as a result. Jot down your thoughts below.

Thank you for doing Bible study with us these weeks. I pray that God will reward you abundantly beyond all that you can ask or think, according to His power that works within you.

TRUE

BETHMOORE

VIEWERGUIDE

The people of God have the power within us, not just to do or to act, but to _____.

      John 14:15-26

The very nature of *agape* love in the Greek New Testament is a love that

is _____.

      John 14:21-23

      John 14:24-27

      1 Corinthians 2:6-16

"We have the _____ of Christ." 1 Corinthians 2:16

God fashioned us for _____.

2 Timothy 3:1

2 Timothy 3:12-13

Do not be _____. (See 1 Cor. 6:9; Gal. 6:7; Jas. 1:16.)

GROUP DISCUSSION QUESTIONS

1. Sometimes we need to know something that we don't. What steps do you take to discern what God wants you to do?

2. In your own words, what is *agape* love? How does God show you *agape* love? How do you demonstrate yours for Him?

WEEK FIVE | DAY ONE
Something for You

The Power Working in Us

Hey, Sister! I'm so honored to walk with you through the next two weeks. Let's pick up where my good buddy, Priscilla, left off. In her fabulous sessions, she talked with us about the power of God working in us. Let's really get specific in this segment about a vital way God can be at work within us. He can supply not only the power to act but also the power to know. Stay with me here and let's see if we can hash this out together.

God is perfectly capable of supplying you and me with the power to know what we cannot humanly know. In fact, one way you can be sure that God is at work is when He supplies your need to discern what you cannot clearly see.

As I shared with you in the session, I suspect we both come against challenges and circumstances where we need to know something that we simply do not. Simply cannot. How often do you find yourself in a situation where you need discernment to do what God wants you to do? How in the world are we supposed to live victoriously in unclear circumstances and know how to respond when the whole situation is cloudy and subjective? How are we to take the next step when it's not black and white? In this moment, in this season of time, do you find yourself living in that gray zone? We're going to discover how a divine power works within us to know what to do when the answer is not in black and white on the sacred page. We have to rely on another means to discern exactly what to do.

Begin with prayer. Ask God to enlighten your mind to His Word. Then look at the Scripture and respond to the questions.

Read John 14:15.
How would you explain to a new believer the relationship between "knowing" and "obedience"?

What part does loving Christ—not just knowing or believing in Him—
play in recognizing what to do or how to obey Him?

You might recall that we strongly emphasized John 14:21 as one of our key verses for this segment. Take another look at it. "He who loves me will be loved by my Father, and I too will love him and show myself to him."

As you evaluate your life, in what ways does your obedience to God's Word positively demonstrate that you love Him?

Does God Love Conditionally?

Perhaps you recall me sharing with you that if I were new to the Word of God, John 14:21 would form a very large question mark in my mind. I'd be thinking, *Isn't the first thing we learn John 3:16, "For God so loved the world"?* I thought there was nothing we could do to make Him love us more than He already does. Didn't you? Is John 14:21 saying that if I'm obedient to Him and if I have affection for Him He's going to love me more? To our great relief, no, it doesn't.

Let's explore what the text is conveying. The very nature of *agape* love in the Greek New Testament (the word that is translated here in John 14:21) is a love that is demonstrative. *Agape* encompasses a love that is shown.

Jesus wasn't saying that He only loves those who love Him. He was saying the more you obey and set your affections on Him, the more He is loosed to disclose Himself to you and the more He can demonstrate His love to you.

Those of us who are parents can surely understand the process and those of us who aren't won't have trouble grasping it. Think of all those times we've continued to say to an out-of-control child, "OK, that's enough. I said that's enough!" If they don't respond, don't we often end up yelling something like, "I've had it! Stop it or else!"?

That's invariably when they respond with a sulk as if we've injured them for life. "You are so mean. Why do you have to yell?"

Sound familiar? Does it count that we said it nicely 45 times? But how different is it when your children were obedient and their hearts were tender before you, the parent? Ah, suddenly you feel free to demonstrate all sorts of love to them. Are you tracking with me? That's the picture Jesus gave in John 14:21, "The one who loves me will be loved by my Father, and I too will love him and show myself to him."

How does it feel when you can look back at an event and know you immediately acted in obedience to God's command?

What benefits does Psalm 37:30-33 describe coming from prompt obedience?

In Psalm 49:3-4, what steps did the psalmist take to help him understand and obey God?

What concrete steps could you take to emulate the psalmist ...

—to meditate and gain understanding?

—to listen to God speak through His Word?

Demonstrative Agape Love

Let's echo the concept again and continue to widen it: The very nature of *agape* love in the Greek New Testament is a love that is demonstrative. It's a love that is shown. Glance at Romans 5:8 for yourself. How does this verse perfectly illustrate the concept?

Agape is a love of the will and not only the emotions. *Agape* undoubtedly includes an emotional love as well, but the will is perhaps its most important driver. We're paraphrasing Christ's meaning in John 14:21 like this: Jesus said, "Listen, listen to Me, the more you obey Me and set your affections on Me, the more I am loosed to disclose Myself to you. The more I can demonstrate My love to you." If God demonstrated His love to you using the same measure of expression that you demonstrate your love for Him, how would your life differ?

How does knowing that God loves you with an *agape* type of love affect your willingness to obey Him?

WEEK FIVE | **DAY TWO**

His Dwelling Place

A Place for Him

With your permission I'll try to sum up Christ's words to His disciples in John 14 in terms we can wrap our minds around. He said, "I'm going to prepare a place for you and until our place is prepared, I'm going to, in effect, still live life out on this planet by living with and through you. Through My Holy Spirit I'm going to make Myself at home on earth with you while I'm making you a home in heaven with Me." This is how He dwells in our generation this side of the cross. Yes, He dwells on this earth through His omniscient Spirit everywhere at all times, but He also resides here on this terrestrial sod through the very vessels of believers.

Read John 16:1-15 and respond to the following questions:

Why do you think Jesus told His disciples that it was to their advantage that He go away?

Have you ever been like the disciples, thinking, *I'd be a whole lot better off if Christ were here in the flesh to help me rather than appreciating His presence through His Holy Spirit?* Me too! Name the most recent time.

What attributes of the Holy Spirit are revealed in verses 7-15?

What role does the Holy Spirit play in our understanding of God's Word and commands (v. 13)?

How can understanding verse 13 encourage you in your pursuit of knowing more about God and His Word?

What advantages do we have as believers as the dwelling place of the Holy Spirit versus having Him only in a temple or structure?

What aspects of the Holy Spirit's presence in your life do you recognize the most?

What aspects of the Holy Spirit's presence in your life do you most struggle to understand or implement?

A Revolutionary Change

What a revolutionary change—that no longer would the Holy Spirit dwell around them but literally in them! In the entire Old Testament we have record of only about 100 people under the direct power of the Holy Spirit, either filled or anointed by Him. So, prior to the cross the Holy Spirit did not operate by dwelling in every child of God. Christ came, gave His life, and was resurrected from the dead so that He could ascend to the right hand of God and send His very Spirit to dwell in us the moment we are saved.

Read 1 Corinthians 3:16-17 and respond to the following:

In what positive ways does your life reflect your understanding that as a child of God, His Holy Spirit resides in you?

In what areas do you long for the presence of His Spirit to be reflected more vividly in your life?

Name a few reasons why you think Satan would love to confuse believers about the indwelling of the Holy Spirit.

How can 1 Corinthians 3:16-17 encourage you to treat your body appropriately as a temple of the Holy Spirit?

How does 1 Corinthians 6:12-20 contradict the thought that *It's my body, I can do what I want with it?*

Describe how you help a new believer understand the importance of a lifestyle that honors her body as the temple of the Holy Spirit.

WEEK FIVE | DAY THREE
Spiritual Discernment

The Mind of Christ

First Corinthians 2:15 states, "The spiritual man makes judgments about all things"—not all people, mind you, all things. "But he himself is not subject to any man's judgment: 'For who has known the mind of the LORD that he may instruct him?' But we have the mind of Christ" (vv. 15-16).

Just let that sit on you. It's so exciting that it's nearly alarming. We, the people of God, have the very mind of Christ. Our challenge is to learn how to activate His mind in our thought processes regarding the reality of our experience. Let's concentrate in this lesson on how to become spiritually discerning.

We need few things more in our generation than we need spiritual discernment. We need to know what to do, how to proceed, and how to respond when a situation is not black and white. I promise you in the authority of Christ's Word and His great name many things are going on around us that are not visible to us. That's the reason why everything's not just cut and dried for us. There may be much more going on in your situation than you know. Something down through the generations may be greatly and positively impacted because of your experience now. Big things, beloved. Things for the glory of God, things for the good of man. For those kinds of results, we've got to know some things that we simply do not know.

In your own words, define *spiritual discernment.*

On a scale of 1 to 10 (1 representing little and 10 representing much), how spiritually discerning do you think you might be? _____ Explain your answer. Perhaps, like me, you've blown it recently and questioned if you have any at all. On the other hand, you might have seen something coming when no one else was aware of it. Don't feel awkward about explaining your self-evaluation.

What do you think often prevents us from sharpening our discernment?

Use 1 Corinthians 2:6-16 and 1 Corinthians 3:18-23 to answer the following questions:

What do you see as the relationship between spiritual discernment and obtaining wisdom?

How does the wisdom obtained through spiritual discernment differ from the wisdom of this world?

What role does spiritual discernment play in our having the mind of Christ?

Delighting in Wisdom

The Lord delights in our pursuit of His wisdom and His discernment. His great desire is for us to know Him more fully. The Old Testament gives us an example of a king who was offered the chance to ask whatever he wanted from the Lord, and he chose wisdom. See for yourself, even if the story is very familiar to you. You might receive a brand-new insight.

Read 1 Kings 3:5-14 and answer the following questions:

What was Solomon's request from the Lord? For what purpose did he desire this (v. 9)?

What was God's response to Solomon's request?

No Accidental Discernment

No one becomes spiritually discerning by accident. We grow in our discernment through prayer, pursuit, and practice. Because we possess the indwelling Holy Spirit, each of us in Christ possesses the potential for great discernment. The capacity is always there. Sometimes it's simply like a muscle that needs to be exercised to grow stronger.

How does Hebrews 5:11-14 describe the difference between those trained and untrained in spiritual discernment?

According to verse 14, what should be our personal practice toward discernment?

The apostle Paul knew the value of spiritual discernment personally. He considered it important enough to make a special mention of it in his letter to the Philippian believers.

Use Philippians 1:1-11 to discuss the following questions:

What was Paul's specific prayer for these believers?

For what purpose did Paul pray this for the believers?

How does this prayer demonstrate that even if we are doing well in our spiritual lives, we should always be seeking to sharpen our spiritual discernment?

Punked

A Painful Realization

Remember when I told my ministry companions everything that had happened concerning the woman who'd duped us and my friend Rich went totally dead silent? Unlike yours truly sometimes, Rich is a thinker and actually tries to process a thought before he speaks. Sounds like a wise man to me. As I described to you, after a silent moment or two, he blurted from the driver's seat, "We've been punk'd."

He was right! Suddenly I knew what to call it. We'd been punk'd! Now it's your turn on the hot seat next to me, so scoot right on over here: Has anybody but me ever been punk'd by the Devil?

Oh, let me tell you. Getting punk'd can cost you. You can get punk'd, and it can be the end of your marriage. Don't tell me you don't need spiritual discernment. You can get punk'd and can get into the biggest mess of your life in your occupation because you became partners with somebody you shouldn't have. Everything seemed fine on the surface, only you had that feeling in your spiritual gut that something seemed off and didn't listen to it.

Have you experienced a time when you have been punked by someone? 'Fess up! I need the company! What were the circumstances?

How did the deceit cause you to feel?

Did the deceit affect your relationship with God at the time? How so?

Examples All Around Us

Imagine all the scenarios. Or maybe, like me, you don't have to imagine. You have that feeling about your teenager's boyfriend. He says all the right things, but you just have that feeling that he's bad news. Untrustworthy. Does this speak to you in any way? Maybe it's not your teenager or relative in that suspicious relationship. Maybe it's you. Perhaps you just had that feeling on that date … just something about it brought up an invisible flag. Listen, there are plenty of ways to tell if you've been punk'd. Anybody ever been betrayed? misled? Anybody besides me ever been just flat out taken advantage of? taken for a fool, anybody? Just duped and flat-out lied to.

It's awful to be punk'd, but take heart. It is not uncommon. Have you looked back on something and been furious at yourself because you knew you had a flag in the beginning and you talked yourself out of it? Surely someone besides me has talked herself right out of going with your gut. Every single one of us needs to know how to go with God through that feeling in our spiritual gut and develop some real live discernment. This could be the salvation of marriages, of friendships, partnerships, and certainly of our churches.

Take this, for example: What if the deacon body, the elders, or the pastor and the staff were onto something that was beginning to take rapid seed in the congregation? Maybe they couldn't quite put their finger on what seemed out of kilter. Perhaps everything seemed OK on the outside but somehow something was unsettling on the inside. What if they talked themselves out of dealing with it because they hated to upset everybody? Or couldn't quite prove what was wrong with it? Can you imagine the repercussions and the regrets? Listen carefully, church leadership: Revival can sometimes be as much about the people who leave as well as it is the people who come. Sometimes when you're going to make folks mad just by speaking the truth and taking the God-given authority placed in your hands, a few people leaving may not be the worst-case scenario.

Without indicting anyone or betraying a confidence, when was the last time your spiritual gut told you to do something or avoid something? How did you respond?

When was the last time you regretted not following your spiritual gut in a situation?

What was the outcome, and what did you learn?

I want you to lock in on 2 Timothy 3:12-13. Notice where it says, "In fact, everyone who wants to live a godly life in Christ Jesus will be persecuted." Kay described this painful reality in our first session. Without a doubt we are facing a heated and intensifying persecution. We can count on it. We've got to be ready.

But notice the words in verse 13, "While evil men and impostors will go from bad to worse, deceiving and being deceived." Do you see it? As time goes on and the birth pains get closer together, we are getting further along on that kingdom calendar between the two advents. We're getting closer to the second coming of Christ than the first coming of Christ. As we grow closer and closer to the day of all days, impostors will multiply, and we had better be ready for them. Many of them are frighteningly good at their jobs.

How can 2 Timothy 3:12-13 prepare you for times of deceit?

Read the following passages of Scripture and describe how each teaches us an important lesson about God and deceit.

Galatians 6:7

James 1:16

Luke 21:8

How we react to being punked is of utmost importance. Rather than running away from God angry and upset, let's learn to run to Him for protection and comfort.

Use Psalm 71 to describe the blessings and benefits of running to God when we have been deceived.

How can you use this psalm to remind yourself not to run away from God when you feel betrayed by someone or a situation?

Our Need to be Significant

We have countless opportunities in this information age to be fooled. Have you ever been duped on a blog? Have you ever gotten emotionally involved in a story line only to find out later that wasn't even real? I love social networking as much as many of you, but let's admit it: This information age offers people untold opportunities to contrive completely fictional characters on Web sites, advertisements, blogs, Facebook accounts, and Twitter. That doesn't mean we drop out of all forms of social networking. It means we start listening when something deep inside of us tells us a story doesn't add up. I'm not suggesting we blow whistles, especially when we're unsure, but we certainly can consider distancing ourselves from a situation that seems consistently questionable. If we can't shake the feeling, let's shake off the tie. We are inhabitants of planet Earth in the age of the poser. We must learn how to discern the difference between truth and lies.

Here's a question that occurs to me as we consider how many posers are out there: Do all those occurrences suggest anything to us about how desperate humans are for significance? This is one reason why we need to know our significance. It's such a crucial soul need that we could end up making up our significance like so many people online. We'd better know who we are in Christ. We were fashioned for significance. We were created in the image of God, and there's something in us, something deep in the human soul, that needs to matter. If we don't make the discovery in truth, we will twist off and find a way to be significant in some way that is unholy and carnal and most likely deceptive in one form or another. That's how much we need it. That's how much we yearn for it.

When do you tend to feel most significant and what's driving it at that time?

How have you, like me and like most of us, sought significance in places other than your relationship with the Lord?

How temporary did it turn out to be?

All we have to do is go back to the Book of Beginnings, the fascinating Book of Genesis, to find the amazing foundation for our unique significance as humans. God waited no longer than the very start to show us what a spectacular place and plan He had for His prized creation.

Search Genesis 1:26-31 and list every inference to our significance and our distinction from the rest of creation.

All throughout Scripture God gives us reminders that our significance is to be sourced in our relationship to Him. When we seek it outside of Him, we are doomed to disappointment. Finding it in Him, however, finally provides us a permanent foundation.

Use the following passages of Scripture to describe the various ways we can find our true significance in our relationship with the Lord through Jesus Christ.

John 1:12

1 Corinthians 6:17

Ephesians 1:5

Ephesians 2:18

Colossians 2:10

Unfortunately, the temporary poser isn't always somebody else. Sometimes it's us. Chances are, somebody reading this study guide knows exactly what I'm talking about. Even at this very season of your life, you may secretly be posing as someone you are not. Don't shrink back, sister, or cast yourself into a ditch of self-condemnation. Trust me on this one. I've been there in my past. People who come from my kind of background are great at posing. Of all the areas of bondage God has freed me from, I'm not sure any of them has been a greater relief to cast away from my life than inauthenticity. Or let's just call it what it was for me: hypocrisy. It's a miserable way to live.

> How have you ever posed as someone you are not in an attempt to feel important?

> What are other ways besides those we've mentioned that people pose as someone they are not in attempts to feel significant?

Let's wrap this section up with a little review and a little more truth. We've established that you and I are occupants on planet Earth in an unprecedented information age, and with the increase of information comes an increase of deception. We don't have to live as victims. We can learn how to refrain from falling for it. We might as well go ahead and welcome one another to the era of the poser and to bid one great caution as we live daily life in our culture. Let's learn how to protect ourselves and our families.

> Read 2 Timothy 3:1-9. List every way our modern "era of the poser" relates to the ungodliness described in these verses.

In your own words, why do you think posing is so appealing to some people? We've already established our need for significance. What additional motivators might it have?

Expand on ways you could guard yourself in the midst of social networking online.

When we pose or use deceit to earn a sense of significance, our pretend Humpty Dumpty is going to have a great fall. It's inevitable. We are ultimately doing ourselves great harm and others a serious disservice. Jesus Christ not only tells us truth, He is truth (John 14:6). Therefore, when we walk away from truth, we are walking toward the agenda of a dangerous enemy with a plan to kill, steal, and destroy.

How do both Genesis 3:1 and 2 Corinthians 11:14 suggest that Satan is the ultimate poser?

In conclusion, how does Ephesians 4:25 speak to you about the importance of truth during this "age of the poser"?

Thank you for your willingness to search your own heart and propensity toward being deceived or deceiving. These are frightening days in many ways, yet you and I were specifically timed by God to be servants in this generation. We can do this victoriously with His might and integrity! Furthermore, getting punk'd isn't the worst thing that could happen … if it causes us to wise up. May God use His Word to open our eyes and strengthen our defenses in this world of posers.

The Pull of ~Riptide~ Friendships

{ Are you in a relationship that's dragging you far from where you need to be spiritually and emotionally? }

By Camerin Courtney

IN FRIENDSHIP, AS IN SWIMMING, it hits you by surprise. Everything seems fine on the surface. Then suddenly a powerful force sweeps you far away from where you want to be—a riptide.

With swimming, a riptide's strong undercurrent carries you dangerously far from shore. In friendship, a riptide relationship pulls you away from where you want to be emotionally and spiritually.

Either way, this mighty flux leaves you adrift—wondering how something innocent could become so destructive—and eager to find your way back to solid ground.

Recognizing the Riptide

No friend or friendship is perfect, so how do you know when you're in a riptide relationship?

"If your friend is dependent on you rather than on God, that's a big riptide sign," says Cheryl Baird, a licensed professional counselor and the director of women's ministries at a Chicago-area church.

Cheryl lists good questions to ask about the friendship: *Does your friend get jealous when you're friends with others? Does your friend exert a lot of control over your friendship? Does she express depression or anger if you're unavailable, even if it's for a legitimate reason? Does your friend feel like a bottomless pit of emotional need?*

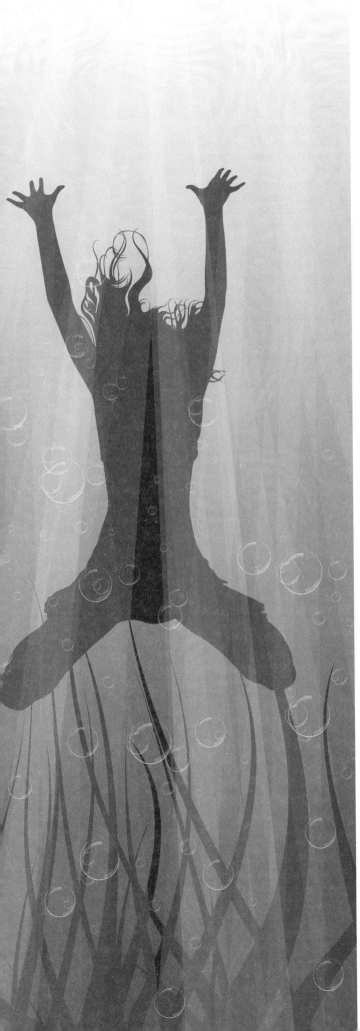

If you answer "yes" to most of these questions, you're likely in a riptide relationship.

Amie, a 30-something single mom, met her riptide friend, Joan, in a Bible study. At first, the friendship seemed like a positive force in Amie's life. When Amie was struggling with self-confidence, Joan helped by asking a simple question: *"Where's God in this situation?"*

But over time, Joan became more and more controlling. She would get angry if Amie called when she didn't want her to. She told Amie how much she could e-mail her, even though she sometimes e-mailed Amie daily.

"In a healthy friendship, there's mutual give and take; but in a riptide relationship, one person does most of the giving. There's not the sense that both people have the other's best interests at heart," explains counselor Mari Skura. When you're in a riptide friendship, she adds, you feel drained, stressed, or angry after spending time together, rather than enriched and supported.

Drained is exactly how Cassandra felt whenever she'd talk with her church friend Tina. Both women suffered from eating disorders, but Cassandra was further along in her recovery. She felt the need to be the strong one, especially when Tina called every day wanting to talk about her problems.

One day, exhausted, Cassandra wrote in her journal, *The oppressive weight of Tina's despair tips me over the edge. I know you can shoulder the weight, God, but I can't. I cannot fight her battles and mine. I can't fix her.*

Confronting Grace Myths

Christians can be acutely susceptible to riptide relationships because of the high value placed on grace and forgiveness. This was certainly the case with Amie. Because the friendship started so well and because, as Amie says, "I wanted to give this friend grace," it took her a while to realize Joan was a riptide in her life.

Many Christians stay in unhealthy friendships out of a sense of obligation, Mari explains. "But if you're only staying in the friendship because you'd feel like a bad Christian if you got out, that's an unhealthy sign."

Several Bible verses also create confusion about riptide friendships and fuel hesitancy to walk away from them—either temporarily or permanently: We know a friend loves at all times (Proverbs 17:17), that true love involves laying down our life for our friends (John 15:13), that we're called to do all we can to live at peace with others (Romans 12:18).

"Sometimes you lay down your life for a friend by setting a difficult boundary," Cheryl asserts. "*Agape* love releases a friend to be all she can be in Jesus; it's saying to her, 'I'm not available, but tell me about the time you spent with Jesus this week. How is He meeting your needs?'" Cheryl adds.

"There are times when you love [someone] best by walking away," Cheryl explains. "If you've become the focal point and are therefore pulling her away from God, you need to take a step back."

Swimming to Safety

In an ocean riptide, swimmers are advised not to struggle against the current, but to remain calm, conserve energy, and swim parallel to the shore. In a friendship riptide, a similar strategy involves pulling back from the friendship, not being as available to your riptide friend, and praying that God will fill those extra spaces in her life (and yours). But you have to communicate with your friend about what you're doing because a needy or possessive friend might latch on harder if she senses you slipping away.

Find time to talk alone together and first name the good in your friend and in the friendship. "Then be honest, and list the qualities of the relationship that aren't healthy," Mari suggests. "Say, 'I can't provide what you're needing from me. I don't want to be the focal point. The focal point needs to be Jesus Christ, so I need to step back.'"

{ **Many Christians stay in unhealthy friendships out of a sense of obligation.**

Amie decided to break up with her friend Joan when she realized the friendship had become a drain. Joan had moved out of state by this time and told Amie not to call her for a month, so Amie sent her a letter. "I told her, 'I'm really sad to say this, but I can't be your friend if this is the way you're going to treat me.' I haven't heard from her since."

Though Cassandra was young at the time of her riptide friendship with Tina and their unhealthy dependency lessened naturally over time, Cassandra says she's learned some valuable lessons from how others have responded to her when she's been too needy. "One friend said to me, 'I want to be one of the people in your support network, but I can't be the only one.' I wish I would have had the wisdom to say that — and mean it — with Tina."

When giving each other space, either temporarily or for good, do so with prayer. Entrust your friend to God's all-powerful, ever-loving care. And pray for healing from your own loss. As Sarah Zacharias Davis writes in her book *The Friends We Keep* (WaterBrook Press), "Recovering from the breakup of a friendship requires healing. To be friends necessitates trust, honesty, and — the hardest of all — vulnerability. It's easy to feel like friendships that get away snatch a piece of us with them. But they leave something with us too. More than disappointment, hurt, or wounds, they leave the experiences of shared emotions, events, conversations, and wisdom folded into the creases in our lives, enriching them with texture."

Embracing the Beauty of True Friendship

Even with all the complications, friendships are so worth the effort. Ecclesiastes 4:9 tells us that "two are better than one." C.S. Lewis wisely said, "Friendship is unnecessary, like philosophy, like art … It has no survival value; rather it is one of those things that give value to survival."

"We are definitely created to be in community, especially we women," says Cheryl. And these friends—the healthy

Are YOU the riptide friend?

ASK YOURSELF:
▶ Do I move this friend toward myself or toward Jesus?
▶ Am I constantly analyzing the friendship?
▶ Am I unwilling to share this friend's time with others?
▶ Does the thought of not speaking to this friend for a few days or weeks make me panic?
▶ Is maintaining this relationship requiring more time than I'm able to spend with God?

If you answered "yes" to most of these questions, it's time for a change. Here are a few steps to get you started:

1▶ Dream dreams for your friend that have nothing to do with you. "True friendship launches friends out to experience all God has for them," asserts counselor Cheryl Baird. Make some sacrifices to help your friend realize her potential, such as watching her kids while she takes a class.

2▶ Pray with your friend to invite God into your relationship. Pray that you'll draw each other closer to God and that He will help you break unhealthy patterns.

3▶ Fast from your friend. Vow to call only once a week instead of daily. "Ask God to fill in those spaces your friend used to occupy," Cheryl says.

4▶ Read great resources. Mari suggests *Safe People* and *Boundaries* by Drs. Henry Cloud and John Townsend (Zondervan). Or try *The Friendships of Women* by Dee Brestin (David C. Cook) or *The Friends We Keep* by Sarah Zacharias Davis (WaterBrook Press).

---

ones—enrich our lives. "Each time I talk with my friend Sonia, I know Jesus better because of something she asked."

True friendships are marked by that kind of mutual spiritual encouragement. By open-handedness and inclusivity. By grace and forgiveness as a first response. By an attitude of giving, not taking. By a desire to see the other person reach her potential. And by honesty.

Cheryl says, "I read a great quote once: 'Build a bridge of friendship strong enough to sustain the weight of truth.' I love the idea that there's room in the friendship for honesty, and it won't snap the relationship in half.

"For example, earlier today I talked with a friend about something she'd said that hurt me. Rather than getting defensive, she received my words and said, 'OK, this is a way God is forming me.' To me, that's a sign of a healthy friendship. It keeps short accounts and doesn't let things pile up." Or morph into a riptide.

Amie recently had an interaction with a newer, healthier friend that underscored the difference between a riptide relationship and real friendship. A third party had falsely accused Amie of betraying this friend's confidence. While Amie's immediate reaction was fear of losing the friendship, the friend responded with grace and trust. "She said, 'Amie, I know you. If you say you didn't do this, I know you didn't. And even if you had, I'd still be your friend.' And I thought, *This is what it should be.* True friendship can happen. And it's healing." Because at its best, it mirrors the greatest Friend of all. □

Camerin Courtney, *a writer living in the Chicago suburbs, is grateful for her friends — especially those she can talk with for hours over steaming cups of coffee. Visit her at camerincourtney.com.*

The skinny jeans were not an option today.

HomeLife can't squeeze you into your favorite jeans,

but we can help you deepen your faith, strengthen your relationships, and manage your life. What other magazine does all that?

For more information, to subscribe, or to place a group order for your church, visit lifeway.com/homelife or call 800.458.2772.

VIEWERGUIDE

TWO DIMENSIONS OF SPIRITUAL REVELATION WE DESPERATELY NEED:

1. Divine revelation in our _____ encounters

Can I trust what I'm sensing?

    1. Am I a _____ or _____ person by nature?

    2. Am I _____ or do I feel _____?

    3. Do I have anything _____ to _____ from this outcome?

    4. Are my _____ clouding my discernment?

You cannot walk in the Spirit and not have a heavy-duty _____ with Christ.

The Spirit fills us to the extent that we yield to His _____.

We will never live a day in the Spirit _____.

Based on these four questions, we needed four no's to make a *yes*:

    1. Am I a critical or suspicious person by nature?
    2. Am I jealous or do I feel threatened?
    3. Do I have anything selfish to gain from this outcome?
    4. Are my emotions clouding my discernment?

The yes is the Holy Spirit is _____ me something.

Listen for one of four instructions from God:

1. _____

2. Take a _____ _____.

3. Ask questions. Confront in person if the Spirit leads you in this direction.

4. _____ _____, but love with your eyes wide open.

Obadiah 1:3
Psalm 116:11

2. Divine revelation in our _____ encounters

John 14:21

Christ wants to give us enlightened hearts that can _____ Him and _____ Him at work.

GROUP DISCUSSION QUESTIONS

1. How should the fact that God is always in control affect how we relate to others?

2. When we've been burned enough, we could be tempted to love less and less. What can we do to learn how to love with knowledge and insight?

WEEK SIX | DAY ONE
Am I Critical by Nature?

We've been talking about letting the mind of Christ work in our minds. If you're like me, you could use all the supernatural insight and wisdom God is willing to give you. We need some divine revelation in our human encounters. Here's one major catch: if we don't know God's Word, we have no way of knowing if what we're sensing is from God or from our own human natures. If we're walking with God in His Word and we are sensing something in our spirit, something deep inside of us, then we need to ask ourselves some questions to figure out whether or not we can trust what we're feeling.

I think this subject is fascinating precisely because we're talking about those things that fall into the gray zone. Situations and decisions that are not black and white. Before we go any further, I'd love to hear from you.

> Up to now, how have you known whether or not you could trust what you were sensing?

> What guidelines have you used in recent years to discern if you were sensing something from the Lord or if it was coming from your own notions?

I want to pitch out four primary questions that you and I can ask ourselves to help us determine whether we can trust what we're calling our spiritual gut.

For us to trust an inner sense on an issue that is not crystal clear in God's Word, we need a "no" answer to these four questions. Think of it like this: Four "no's" make a "yes." In other words, based on these four no's, yes, I can mostly likely trust what I'm sensing. Here's the first one: *Am I a critical or suspicious person by nature?*

Self-evaluations have a natural leaning toward inaccuracy because we tend to have so many blind spots when we look in the mirror. We'll grapple with a few underlying questions to get to the bottom of each of our four primary ones. Each will take utmost honesty:

Is your typical first reaction to something trust or criticism? Why do you think that's your tendency?

How have you discerned the difference between the leading of the Holy Spirit and the criticism coming from your own nature?

Our natures are strong. They can pose as God and we can end up thinking that anything we feel strongly enough could only come from Him. The inclination of the human nature is to exalt itself and pretend to be God. Therefore, I can't automatically conclude that, based on how much I feel a certain way, God is the one putting it in my heart. Never forget that our emotions and our intellects can be overcome with deception. Later in the week we'll see Jeremiah 17:9 and 2 Corinthians 11:2. Both of these support the previous statement. Left to ourselves, we can become utterly convinced of something that is utterly false.

Describe a situation in which your critical nature was so strong that you missed, or almost missed, hearing the voice of the Lord.

Why do you think it is important to reconcile whether we are being critical out of our nature about a decision or if the Lord is directing us away from the situation?

What does James 4:1-3 say about how our nature can pose as God yet cause fights and quarrels when not correctly handled?

The flesh can be strong. That's why we must begin our evaluation by asking ourselves, "Am I a critical or suspicious person by nature?" Listen, if somewhere along the way you and I earned the tendency not to trust people, we're going to automatically transfer that response to all sorts of situations that don't warrant it.

At the risk of stating the obvious, if we don't trust anybody, we'll cast suspicion on everybody. I write these words with empathy: If you don't trust anyone, you can't trust your discernment because you can't even trust yourself. Do you understand what I'm saying?

So, that's why we've got to look carefully at our first primary question, Am I a critical or suspicious person by nature? We need a "no" answer to that very important question.

So, with some discussion behind us to clarify the issues, do you tend to be a critical or suspicious person by nature? If so, why or why not?

Plan to talk with your group about strategies those with a suspicious nature can use to improve their decision making.

In what way can a personal critical/suspicious nature impede you from hearing God's direction?

What role does pride play in a critical attitude?

How do you think we could go about allowing God to transform something so innate in us as a life-long critical nature?

On dealing with numerous situations that would have caused most of us to become critical or suspicious, we might find some help in knowing that Job had moments when he too became suspicious. The astonishing admission is that a certain measure of his doubt can be construed toward the Lord. The Book of Job provides ample verses revealing the heart and life of a man whose faith was tested beyond what many could endure. While God patiently allowed Job to work out his faith and doubts, He did answer Job directly when the criticism was cast toward Him.

In your own words, what was God's response to Job's doubts and criticism in Job 38?

Do you think God might be trying to remind you, like He did Job, that He is the source of all wisdom, discernment, and knowledge about some matter? If so, how?

After hearing the word of the Lord in response to his doubts, Job quickly repented and reminded himself that although he may not always understand a situation, God is always in control.

In Job 42:1-6, what was Job's response to his new faith in God's ultimate wisdom and knowledge?

In what ways can Job set a standard for us in these verses?

Read the following passages and explain how each uniquely speaks of the importance of trusting God and not self.

Psalm 9:10

Psalm 18:30

Psalm 20

Isaiah 12:2

Am I Threatened?

We've established that the first question we need a negative answer to is: *Am I critical or suspicious by nature?* Now let's move to the second question that requires a "no" response: *Am I jealous, or do I feel threatened?*

First Corinthians 3:1-3 says, "Brothers [and sisters], I could not address you as spiritual but as worldly—mere infants in Christ. I gave you milk, not solid food, for you were not ... ready for it. Indeed, you are still not ready. You are still worldly. For since there is jealousy and quarreling among you, are you not worldly? Are you not acting like mere men?"

The magnificent assumption offered in this section of Scripture is this: We are not mere men and women when we're in Christ. That's great news! It's also one less excuse when we'd like to say we couldn't help responding a certain carnal way. The Holy Spirit of the living God dwells within us. We're not like the unredeemed. We don't have to sink to the worldly common denominators of jealousy and covetousness and greed. We're not mere women. We may be simple, fragile jars of clay, but we contain the all-surpassing power of the living Lord Jesus Christ within us.

How does jealousy display immaturity in the Lord?

Why do you think we need to know whether jealousy is playing a role in a decision we are making? Name as many reasons as possible.

Have you ever excused away something the Lord was asking you to do because you were jealous of someone? If so, explain.

How could our jealousy potentially erode our trust in God?

When we have a sudden jealous streak, think of it as a waving red flag. Make a speedy assumption that your human nature is wrapped up in the decision no matter how strong your opinions may be. Is there something I'm jealous of there? Is there something I feel threatened by? Because, you see, our natural tendency—even subconsciously—will be to hope something is wrong with people we're jealous of or feel threatened by. Have you ever experienced what I'm describing? Have you had someone you were jealous of and found yourself naturally looking for something not to like? Isn't that our human nature?

If I've got a jealousy streak going or if I feel threatened by a particular person, I need to run to Jesus as fast as I can. I'll rarely be more prone to false assumptions. Under those heightened conditions, we can't immediately trust what we think we're sensing. We need a "no" answer to the question: *Is my jealousy or fear driving this negative feeling?*

Are you wrestling with jealousy toward someone right now?

How does your jealousy toward that individual affect your ability to discern God's voice?

Can you obey God if He asks you to minister to that person? If so, how?

The only One who can handle jealousy without sin is God. Although this is not a quality we typically associate with God, Scripture repeatedly states that He is indeed a "jealous God." This is right for Him to be so, because He alone deserves all praise, all honor, all respect. His jealousy is sourced out of truth and righteousness. Ours, however, is typically sourced out of pride and distrust.

How do the following verses speak to God's jealousy?

Exodus 20:5

Exodus 34:14

Deuteronomy 5:9

Jealousy in itself does not have to be a bad thing. Note the kind of jealousy the apostle Paul exercised in 2 Corinthians 11:2. Was he jealous *of* someone … or jealous *for* someone?

What would the difference be?

So, here's an underlying question. Is our jealousy *of* someone or *for* someone? When we are jealous *of* someone, we see that person as a threat. Our hearts don't want the best for her. Instead, our personal pride hinders us from loving her as we should. On the other hand, when we are jealous *for* someone, we want nothing more than the best for her.

For example, we may be jealous *for* the well-being of our children and therefore do what we can to ensure that they are taken care of and do not miss out on opportunities. The motive moves from personal pride to concern and care for the other individual.

Without naming the person, describe one challenge you've had over jealousy. What about the person made you feel jealous?

Now name someone you have been jealous *for* and why.

Being jealous *for* someone also creates unity. Unity is the exact opposite of carnal jealousy. In unity, we are looking out for the needs of others as well as our own.

How do the following passages speak to God's desire that we should live in unity?

Psalm 133

Ephesians 4:1-7

Conclude this day of study by asking God to transform your jealousy OF someone into jealousy FOR them. No one has more to gain from the switch than you. After all, if God is for us, who can be against us (Rom. 8:31)?

Do I Have Something to Gain?

So far we've considered the first two of our four primary questions: Do I have a critical nature, and am I somehow threatened or jealous of the person? Remember, in matters of trusting our discernment, four no's make a yes. Here's the third question: *Do I have anything selfish to gain from this outcome?*

If the person proves to be wrong, what would that mean for you? These are questions I have to ask myself. Do I have anything to selfishly gain? What's in it for me, even psychologically? How happy would I be—I am just talking about pure human nature here—if we proved right and they proved a poser, or a liar, or simply not what they seemed? How much satisfaction would it give us if you were right? Or how much credibility might our great discretion win us? Do you get what I'm saying?

We need to ask ourselves if we have anything selfish to gain from proving right. Because if someone looking bad has the capacity to make us look good, spiritual, or wise, then that whole feeling is suspect. Under those conditions, our selfish need or desire to be right throws off true discernment. Even if psychological superiority is our only gain, it is a powerful motivator … and deceiver. Some people just enjoy being right about people being wrong. Is that fair to say? If that's us, it's suspect. We seriously need a "no" answer to the question: Do I have anything selfish to gain from this outcome? And if I've got a "yes" answer, it doesn't always mean I'm totally off base. It means I cannot trust what I'm sensing until I can get my personal agendas and selfish gains out of the middle of it. Until I can honestly say, *No, I don't have anything personal to gain from it,* I can't trust what I feel.

Have you ever been eager to believe you were being led by the Holy Spirit to say or do something, only later to realize your feelings were influenced because you had something to gain from the outcome? If so, explain.

Upon honest reflection, would you have to admit that you have ever even slightly enjoyed being right about people being wrong?

What role can pride play in wanting to say or do something out of selfish gain?

Our pride can get us into so much trouble. Scripture speaks very clearly that when pride enters the picture, trouble is sure to follow.

Write one lesson about pride from each of the following passages:

Proverbs 11:2

Proverbs 16:18

Proverbs 29:23

Jeremiah 49:16

Pride pushes us to desire our best over the best of others. Or it may lead us to begin watching the lives of others so closely that we forget to pay attention to what the Lord wants to be doing in our own lives. We can get so caught up in worrying that someone else is getting something we aren't that we miss out on the special promises God has given personally to us. When we fall into this trap, we begin to stumble into someone else's lane as we run this race of faith.

Girlfriend, you and I better stay in our own lanes. Does anybody besides me tend to keep veering into somebody else's path? Thinking we like their lane, their prospects, their gifts, their opportunities, and their persona better than ours? No wonder we can't run our own races at times. We keep getting distracted by somebody else's. Let's get that foot out of somebody else's lane!

Can you describe a situation in which you stumbled into someone else's lane due to pride or jealousy?

How well were you able to run your own race while having one foot in someone else's lane?

Why do you think women often struggle so hard with the desire to veer into other lanes?

How would your life look different if you were fully engaged in your own race with the Lord and not peering over into others' lives?

Why would Satan love to tempt us constantly to stumble into others' lanes?

Humility assumes the opposite posture from a stance of self-gain. When we seek humility, we lean steadfastly against the temptations Satan places before us. Rather than merely looking out for our own interest, we begin to place the needs of others above our own. In this pursuit, we are less likely to desire to prove someone wrong and more inclined to lift her up and encourage her.

Use Philippians 2:1-18 to answer the following questions:

How do verses 1-2 demonstrate Paul's desire that believers show humility toward one another?

Write the definition of humility provided in verses 3-4.

How well are you currently living out this definition in your life?

Describe the supreme example of humility given to us through the life of Christ (vv. 5-11).

Explain how our obedience to strive toward humility allows us to be "lights to the world" (vv. 12-18).

Are Emotions in My Way?

We've looked at three questions that require a no in order to say yes to our discernment. *Am I critical by nature? Am I feeling threatened or jealous? Do I have something to gain?* Number 4 is this: *Are my emotions clouding my discernment?* I have a feeling God is about to start really meddling in our personal business now. The issue we have before us as we grapple with our fourth primary question is impossible to overstate. As you and I both have discovered numerous times, once our emotions get tangled up in a situation, they can distort the entire picture. They can also take complete charge. Our emotions are God-given. They are gifts shaped from His very image. The objective is not to squelch them. It is to allow God to take authority over them so we can trust them.

In Philippians 1:9-10 Paul said, "This is my prayer: that your love may abound more and more … so that you may approve the things that are excellent" (NASB). In other words, he was saying, "I want you in the authority of Christ, in obedience to His Word, to get more and more loving and not less and less."

We'll be tempted in these days of impostors and deceivers to develop hardness of heart. Any of us burned badly enough is tempted to love less and less. In fact, Matthew 24 says one of the characteristics of the last days will be coldheartedness. Why? One reason will surely be that so much has proved deceptive or destructive that, in pure self-defense, we'll start growing callused and less caring.

OK, let's back up. Can you describe a situation in which your emotions clouded your discernment?

What was the outcome of your decision?

What are some situations that are prime targets for us to allow our emotions to cloud our discernment? Make a list and plan to discuss it with your group this week.

How can our commitment to Philippians 1:9-10 actually
aid and sharpen our discernment even in the midst of
relational challenges?

Paul knew that a heart ever-growing in its capacity to love was the only healthy—
even happy—kind. That's why he prayed "that [our] love may abound more and
more in knowledge and depth of insight, so that [we] may be able to discern
what is best" (NIV). Listen carefully. We're supposed to love more and more,
but girlfriends, we need desperately to learn how to love with knowledge and
insight. No one has loved more foolishly in her past than me. The love of God
is not blind—never, never, never. God's love is wide-eyed open. He's not calling
us to just love blindly. He's calling us to love wisely with insight and knowledge.
But we live in an unprecedented information age, and with the increase of
information, naturally comes an increase of deception. That's just the way it's
going to be.

The love of God is not blind—never, ever. God's love is wide-eyed and
wide-open. He's doesn't call us to just love blindly. He's calling us to love wisely
with insight and knowledge. We are wise to accept that with the increase of
information, naturally comes an increase of deception. That's simply the way it's
going to be. We may feel powerless in the face of mounting deception but we're
not. We are well able to, on the one hand, know truth and teach truth and, on
the other hand, refuse to believe lies or author them. As long as we are aware that
with the increase of information comes the increased potential for deception, we'll
keep our guard up.

Let's continue our discussions on Philippians 1:9-10. How would
you define "loving wisely"?

Do you think women are more tempted than men to let our
emotions drive our relational decisions? Why?

We cannot learn to "love wisely with knowledge" apart from the Word of God. We
must have an intimate relationship with God through His Word and a working
understanding of His precepts to let His Spirit sanctify our emotions. As Christ
prayed to His Father in John 17:17, "Sanctify them by the truth; Your word is
truth." If our emotions are clouded, so then will be our discernment. Therefore,
what we believe to be true will affect how we feel and, in turn, how we feel will
affect our discernment.

Use Hebrews 4:12-13 to describe the critical relationship between knowing God's Word and our ability to discern wisely.

What impact does this verse have on the way we should seek to study and memorize Scripture?

Romans 3:23 reminds us that "all have sinned and fallen short of the glory of God." As long as we are on this earth, we will have to daily deal with our sin nature. This means that we must love wisely and use God's Word, not our emotions, as our source of truth. Although something may feel right to us, we have to realize that we are still capable of sin and therefore deception.

What warning does Jeremiah 17:9 give regarding blindly following our hearts and emotions?

How could you use this verse to council another woman who is attempting to make a poor decision based on something that just "feels right" to her at the time?

We are not left to dangle in confusion over issues. God desires for us to know Him, know His Word, and have wisdom that comes from Him. We risk misunderstanding His counsel when we seek our final answers from ourselves and our feelings rather than from Him.

What promise does Proverbs 3:5-7 give to us regarding wisdom and discernment?

How is this promise tied to the truths found in Hebrews 4:12-13?

Do I Walk By the Spirit?

We've identified and explored the four questions that require a no. To trust our discernment, we need to be able to say:

1. No, my critical nature does not control me.
2. No, I am not feeling threatened or jealous.
3. No, I do not have something to gain by this person being wrong.
4. No, my emotions are not clouding my discernment.

Our original question was, *"Can I trust what I feel or what I believe I'm discerning?"* Four no's to our previous inquiries suggest a yes to our big original question. We are far more liable to affirmatively assume we are walking in the Spirit rather than the flesh. And what a huge relief!

Our present discussion reminds me of the time that the Israelites said something like this to Moses: "You know what? You go talk to God for us because if we talk to him, He'll kill us. We're scared to death of Him. So you go talk to Him, but tell us what He tells you in our behalf and we'll do it" (Ex. 20:19). Translation? "We don't need a real relationship; we can co-exist on rules. Just tell us what to do and we'll do it."

That's how a lot of people still want their religion today. We still say in effect, "I'm not looking to be close to the Father God and get to know Him intimately through His Son Jesus Christ. I just want someone to tell me what to do and what not to do and I'll go on with it from there." The temptation is there because we don't have the burden of relationship with a cold, stony set of laws. What people with this mind-set don't understand is that they're missing the most satisfying love relationship of their entire existence.

Praise God, though, we live this side of the cross and those of us who trust Christ as our personal Savior are no longer bound to the Law. Instead of writing on stone tablets, God writes "on the tablets of human hearts" (2 Cor. 3:3). We live by the law of love as God beckons us to walk by the Spirit and not in the flesh.

In what ways could you allow yourself to be like the people who say, "I'm not looking to be close to the Father God; just tell me what to do and I'll do it"?

What would be easier or comforting about just following rules?

Why do you think God requires of us this side of the cross to walk in the Spirit rather than simply following a set of rules?

How different are the challenges you face in walking by the Spirit versus following a set of established laws/rules? Really think through your response. It's more complicated than it at first seems.

Our present discussions could also raise the following questions: When you or I dwell on our sins and beat ourselves up over our failures, are we walking in the Spirit or living by laws? Why?

Beloved, do you see the ramifications of how we relate to God? We cannot walk in the Spirit and bypass a heavy-duty, all-access, intimate relationship with Jesus Christ. You cannot do it. I cannot do it. No matter how well behaved we are, no matter how healthy our backgrounds, we cannot walk in the Spirit through devotion to legalism. I promise you according to the authority of the Word that dependable discernment comes only by walking in the Spirit, and walking in the Spirit comes only by walking and talking with God Himself. God purposed the system to work exactly this way. It's His way of pushing the envelope of relationship instead of letting us bear all the fruit without an attachment to the Vine. He knows, when all is said and done, we wouldn't have wanted to miss Him for the world. The Spirit of God fills us only to the extent that we yield to His authority and welcome His Presence. We walk with Him to the degree that our affections are tied up with Him and our mind is set on Him. That's why He says so clearly, "'If you love me, you will obey what I command'" (John 14:15).

In the past, how have you tried to walk in the Spirit apart from a personal, intimate relationship with the Lord? What was the result?

What is your biggest hang-up about moving to the next level of relationship with God?

We'll never walk in the Spirit accidentally. Let me say this again more forcefully and not just for your ears but for my own: We will never live one single day in the Spirit accidentally. It simply cannot happen. We will walk in the Spirit only on purpose. I'll put it to you this way: You show me a godly woman, and I'll show you a woman who pursued God.

Though we're not likely to ever frame it this way, do we ever secretly hope to default into the Spirit instead of entering into the relationship with God required? Give an example.

Describe someone you know personally who obviously walks in the Spirit.

What is her pursuit of God like?

The apostle Paul wrote to believers in Galatia about the importance of walking in the Spirit. He gave them a comparison between walking by rules and by the Spirit. Read Galatians 5:16-26 and answer the following questions:

What promise are we given in verse 16 regarding our ability to withstand temptation when we walk by the Spirit?

Describe the relationship between the desires of our flesh and the desires of the Spirit as found in verse 17.

List the desires of the flesh found in verses 19-21.

In what specific ways does the fruit of the Spirit contradict the previously listed desires of the flesh (vv. 22-23)?

Once we have worked through a checklist of our four primary questions and come up with four coinciding no's, we can likely assume that we're walking in the Spirit and God is trying to tell us something. If we still sense a warning from what we're calling our spiritual gut, carefully consider one of four options:

1. Run. Sometimes we need to run from a situation or a person for dear life!
2. Take a step back. Sometimes we simply need to back off a little so that we can think clearer.
3. Speak the truth in love. In other words, lovingly confront. This option is far more effective when we do it face to face.
4. Choose to love with your eyes wide open. Sometimes God may require us to remain in a relationship that is emotionally risky. Sister, spiritually speaking, don't even blink. Philippians 1:9-10 is never more applicable than in these times.

Reflect on those four options. Conclude your week of study with an assignment that will require some time and effort but the rewards and insights will be solid gold. Think back on your journey with God. Describe four separate times when God led you to follow those options. Please don't use names where someone could be dishonored. I want you to be able to share some of your examples with your small group. If, like me, on occasion He led you to take a specific option but you didn't follow it, describe the repercussions under the heading and anything you learned.

A time God told me to RUN:

A time God told me to TAKE A STEP BACK:

A time God told me to CONFRONT THE PERSON AND SPEAK
THE TRUTH IN LOVE:

A time when God told me to remain but to LOVE WITH MY EYES
WIDE OPEN:

Dear Sister, Kay, Priscilla, and I are so honored to be your servants and so grateful
to take this walk of faith with you. Nothing we've ever done earned us the right
to serve people we esteem as highly as you. God's grace alone afforded us this
opportunity. We do not take it lightly. Keep in mind as you go on from here that
walking closely with Him is a goal we will have to pursue all our earthly lives. We
won't always make the right decision even when we have the right motivation.
We'll often feel awkward, unsure, and wobbly on our spiritual feet.

Remember, God looks on our hearts. Not on our performances. Just keep it
real, Sister. Obedience is never harder than in situations that are neither black
nor white. Never forget that He is also God of the gray zone. He knows what He
wants you to do. Keep seeking Him. Choose to die to your own ambitions and
share His aims. James 1:5 says, "If any of you lacks wisdom, he should ask God,
who gives generously to all without finding fault, and it will be given to him."

Hear this at volume 10: Your God loves you so much. His heart alone is so
pure and holy that His emotions never cloud His judgment. His hand is upon
you. As you seek to know Him on the pages of Scripture, He's writing His words
on your very heart. Go with Him, girlfriend. He's a God you can trust.

We love you and believe in God's great work in you.

LEADER GUIDE

Thank you for leading women in Bible study. You will see that Faithful, Abundant, True is both unique and versatile. We sought to plan this resource so you could use it either for a women's retreat/event or for a seven-session Bible study. This leader guide is divided into a retreat plan and a group study plan. You may choose either approach or feel free to create your own version of a combined retreat followed by the study.

Because God often speaks most powerfully to us through example, we have included three articles from *HomeLife* magazine that illustrate the topics Kay, Priscilla, and Beth taught. They may be used as leisure reading along with the content, or you may choose to incorporate discussion of them in your retreat or group sessions. Our prayer is that this effort will challenge and encourage believers to faithfulness, to trust God's ability, and to develop the kind of discernment needed in these difficult last days.

General Suggestions for Your Retreat or Group Study

Adapt these general suggestions to fit your plans. Provide each participant with the book. Activities encourage personal interaction. The study includes six weeks of content—two by each of the authors—with a final meeting to discuss the last week's work and to celebrate, the group will last seven weeks. Each week's material includes five daily lessons, requiring about 30 minutes to read and respond. You can adjust the time to fit your group needs.

In the small-group portion of sessions, women share and discuss what God has taught them from His Word. Small-group sessions build fellowship and relationships, encourage accountability, and multiply the benefits of the study. Women draw closer as they share their thoughts, needs, and prayer concerns.

In the large group women watch the video teaching. Leadership suggestions in this guide reflect the following schedule for the first week. For subsequent weeks the small group will be first, followed by the large group:

Child care (15 min. before session)
Large group—welcome and worship (15 min.)
Large group—video presentation (40 min.)
Break and to small groups (variable time)
Small groups—discussion of the video and past week's work,
    closing assignment, prayer

This guide offers suggestions for leading your group. Adapt it to meet the needs of the women in your church and community. Each small-group leader may also adapt the suggestions to her own style or preferences.

Choosing Leaders

Again, these general guidelines can be adapted either for a weekly study or a retreat. For a retreat you will still need leaders for discussion groups. If you have 12 or fewer women, you need only one leader for both the large and small group. If more women are involved, divide into groups of 8 to 12. You will need a leader for the large group as well as for each small group.

Large-group leader: responsibilities include
  • providing administrative leadership
  • scheduling and promoting the study
  • enlisting small-group leaders
  • ordering resources and distributing books
  • leading the weekly large-group sessions

Small-group facilitators: work with 8 to 12 women to guide discussion
  • stay in contact and encourage their group
  • lead small-group prayer time and pray regularly for participants
  • guide discussion during small-group time
  • follow up on ministry needs

Small-group leaders can use the following suggestions to facilitate discussion.

Before the Session
  • Pray for members by name each week.
  • Do your homework.
  • Pray for God to guide you as you facilitate.
  • Arrange chairs in a circle.

During the Session

- Greet members and start on time.
- Share prayer requests and pray.
- Encourage voluntary sharing. Invite everyone to participate, but make sure no one feels compelled to share personal information beyond her comfort level.
- Be flexible. If women are engaged in meaningful discussion, don't force them to move on just to finish the agenda. On the other hand, don't let one or two women bog down the discussion.
- Share some of your own thoughts and feelings to facilitate discussion. Your example can help women be vulnerable without revealing too many intimate details.
- Whatever women share, show compassion, concern, and support.
- Keep the discussion focused.
- Listen actively by looking at each woman as she speaks and affirm her for sharing.
- Be prepared to lead a participant to faith in Christ.
- End on time. If you see that women want to continue the discussion, consider exchanging e-mail comments during the week.
- Encourage members to do their home study.

After the Session

- Encourage women and follow up on any ministry needs.
- Evaluate the session. Pray for insight and sensitivity to God's Spirit and women's needs.
- Prepare daily for the next session.

Planning Steps

The following steps are suggested to assist the large-group leader.

1. Enlist the support of your pastor.
2. Talk with women in your church. For a retreat, plan together for the best time and schedule. For the study, take a poll to discover whether the study should be offered during the day, the evening, or both.
3. Schedule time on the church calendar.
4. Offer child care, if possible.
5. Estimate the number of participants and order books four to six weeks in advance. If members pay at least part of the cost of their books, they are more likely to attend faithfully and to complete their home study. If you charge for the books, arrange for scholarship funds as needed.
6. Reserve rooms and electronic equipment.
7. Promote the study. Target women in your community who are interested in Bible study. Church bulletins, newsletters, handouts, posters, fliers at Mothers' Day Out, announcements in worship services and in Sunday School classes, phone calls, and word of mouth are excellent and inexpensive ways to promote the study.
8. Pray that God will involve the members He desires and that He will validate this study with His presence and activity in members' lives.

RETREAT PLAN

SUGGESTED FORMAT
Weekend retreat (Friday evening–Saturday evening)

THEME
Relaxed. Casual.

DECORATIONS
Provide comfortable seating in all rooms.
Decorate table tops with candles and/or candy for centerpieces.

DOOR PRIZES
Comfort items (books, favorite snacks, spa gift certificates, women's ministry mugs, tote bags, book marks)

REFRESHMENTS
Snack foods (finger foods provided by the church or brought by participants)

REGISTRATION
As ladies arrive, present them with a name tag. Divide the ladies into three groups using the tags: *Faithful*, *Abundant*, and *True*. These groups will serve as small discussion groups for the weekend. When it is time for discussion groups, have them divide into the three groups consisting of all ladies wearing "Faithful" tag, the "Abundant" tag, and the "True" tag. Allow guests of members to remain with those who brought them if desired.

ROOM SET-UP
VIDEO-VIEWING ROOM: One room large enough to comfortably hold all participants for the group video-viewing time.

DISCUSSION ROOMS: Provide additional smaller rooms for the groups to meet in during the discussion times. One group could remain in the large viewing room if needed. Small groups of 12 or fewer are ideal.

SNACK ROOM: Have one room close to the main viewing room that you can make into a snack room for the weekend. Or, you may choose to arrange some tables in the back of the main viewing room with snacks that will be available for women during the retreat.

MEAL ROOM: Provide access to the fellowship hall or a large banquet room if you host the Saturday lunch and dinner. Other options include: (1) allow the women to leave campus for lunch at local restaurants, or (2) have boxed lunches catered to your retreat site and allow the ladies a casual time of informal discussions and fellowship.

Outline for the Weekend

Friday Evening (3 hours)
1. Welcome/introduction (15 min.)
2. Entire group view video segment for week 1 (45 min.)
3. Discussion of week 1 in small groups. Allow participants to get and eat snacks during this time (30 min.).
4. Entire group view video segment for week 2 (45 min.)
5. Discussion of week 2 in small groups (30 min.)
6. Closing remarks/door prizes. Assign the "I will Carry You" article (p. 129) for devotional reading as an illustration of faithfulness (15 min.).

Saturday Morning (3 hours)
1. Welcome/announcements (15 min.)
2. Entire group view video segment for week 3 (45 min.)
3. Discussion of week 3 in small groups. Allow snacks during this time (30 min.).
4. Entire group will view video segment for week 4 (45 min.)
5. Discussion of week 4 in small groups (30 min.)
6. Announcements/prayer for lunch (15 min.)

Lunch Break (1 hour)

Saturday Afternoon (3 hours)
1. Welcome/announcements (15 min.)
2. Entire group view video segment for week 5 (45 min.)
3. Discussion of week 5 in small groups (30 min.)
4. Entire group view video segment for week 6 (45 min.)
5. Discussion of week 6 in small groups (30 min.)

Closing (90 min.)
Entire group watch panel discussion (45 min.)
Entire group discuss any questions/comments from the panel time (30 min.)
Closing announcements/prayer (15 min.)

Time Schedule for a Two-Day Weekend Format

Friday 6:00 p.m.–9:00 p.m. (Sessions 1 and 2)
Saturday
9:00 a.m–12:00 p.m. (Sessions 3 and 4)
12:00 p.m.–1:00 p.m. (Lunch)
1:00 p.m.–4:00 p.m.(Sessions 5 and 6)
4:00 p.m.–5:30 p.m. (Panel DVD and Discussion)
5:30 p.m.–7:00 p.m. (Dinner and Closing Remarks)

Suggested Questions/ Topics for Small-Group Discussion Times

Discussion times are 30 minutes. Allow 5 minutes for group response to each question. Two group discussion questions appear at the end of each viewer guide. Combine those questions with the following three, and utilize the remaining time for rest room and snack breaks.

1. What most challenged your understanding of God and/or Jesus Christ in this portion of the video?
2. What new aspects of God's character of "faithful, abundant, and true" were revealed to you during this section?
3. What specific questions or concerns came to your mind during the speaker's teaching this session?

Quick Start Checklist (for Retreat or Seven-Session Bible Study)

1. Pray! Before you begin to plan your retreat or weekly Bible study, be sure to pray and seek the Lord's leadership.
2. Obtain approval from your pastor, minister of education, or other staff member who is directly responsible for approving your church's studies and events. Be prepared to present material for their perusal and approval.
3. Gather all needed resources for the event/Bible study, including DVDs for viewing in your large group. Materials may be purchased at a LifeWay Christian Store, by ordering online at *www.lifeway.com*, e-mailing *orderentry@lifeway.com*, calling toll-free 1-800-458-2772, or faxing your order to (615) 251-5933.
4. Encourage input from other women in the church to determine:
   - approximate number of women interested
   - approximate number of children who need child care
   - convenient times and location to meet
5. Enlist a leadership team for the retreat/Bible study.
   - For the Bible study, plan on one facilitator for each small group with no more than 12 in any small group.
   - Conduct preregistration to help determine the number of small groups, but be prepared for women to register at the first meeting.
   - Determine the financial needs of the retreat/Bible study.
6. Nursery care
7. Publicity/Invitations
8. Refreshments/Lunches/Dinners
9. Plan to publicize
   - church newsletter
   - posters
   - city newspapers
   - local Christian radio station
   - flyers
   - church Web site

GROUP STUDY PLAN

SESSION ONE

Before the Session

1. Pray for group members.
2. Read about the three authors (pp. 5-7).
3. Prepare name tags with each having one of the words: *Faithful, Abundant,* or *True*. Mix the tags so women who arrive in groups will get different name tags. Use the tags to divide women into three groups. If you need to divide groups even further, use different color tags. Use these name tags to form the same small groups for the entire seven weeks. Provide markers.
4. Have books ready to distribute.
5. Provide paper and pens or pencils.
6. For the large group meeting place, make three large banners, each with one of these words: *Faithful, Abundant, True*. Display all three during this session; then display only the relevant banner. For the last session, display all three again.
7. Make sure arrangements have been made to secure and set up necessary equipment.
8. If you have more than one small group, arrange for an appropriate number of rooms plus one room large enough for all participants in the large-group session. If you have only one group, you may use the same room for both discussion and viewing the video.
9. Preview the video.
10. Note that in this first session women will view the video in large group and then proceed to their small groups. In subsequent sessions they will meet in small groups to discuss the week's study before proceeding to the large group for the video.
11. You have LifeWay's permission to make copies of the viewer guides for drop-ins or for those who are waiting for a member book.

During the Session (Large Group)

1. Welcome women as they arrive. Ask them to make name tags.
2. Ask women to find someone they don't know well and share one reason they have come to this Bible study.
3. Introduce yourself and other leaders. Create a casual, nonthreatening atmosphere. Suggest that they pray for one another throughout the next seven weeks.
4. Introduce the first video of Kay Arthur teaching from the Book of Hebrews. Direct the women to turn to the viewer guide for session 1 in their books. Provide copies of the viewer guide pages for drop-ins or for those who are waiting for a member book. Make sure they have pens or pencils. Show the first video session.
5. Explain that the next six weeks will begin with the small group first. Direct women to their small groups.

Small Group

1. Spend a few minutes helping group members get to know each other. You might ask each to share something significant about herself that others may not know. Or you may choose to explain that in these sessions we will be exploring three core attributes of God. In their lives, which do they value most: God's faithfulness, His abundance, or His truth? Why?
2. Invite women to brainstorm all that they know about the Book of Hebrews. If possible, make notes on a chalkboard or tear sheets. Note that scholars differ about the author and circumstances of writing, but Hebrews was written to Jewish Christians who, because of persecution, were tempted to turn their backs on Christ. Hebrews lifts up the greatness and supremacy of Christ. It warns against turning from Christ.
3. Talk about the group discussion questions from the viewer guide (p. 11).
4. Explain that each week the workbook days will further explore and "unpack" what Kay, Priscilla, and Beth teach in the sessions. Then each week the small group will discuss what they have learned. Encourage members to do the daily Bible study in their books.
5. Close in prayer. Thank God for the lessons women will learn. Thank Him that He is Faithful, His provision is Abundant, and His Word is True.

SESSION 2

Before the Session
1. Pray for each of your group members.
2. Preview the video and answer the questions in the book for week 1.
3. Provide name tags, pencils, and books as needed.
4. If you have multiple groups, have someone assigned to direct the women to begin with the small group.

During the Session (Small Group)
Emphasis: The Word of God equips us to deal with suffering and prepares us for the days ahead with spiritual maturity.

1. Choose from the following questions to review the week's study.
- Why are Matthew 4:2-4; 2 Timothy 3:16-17; and 2 Peter 1:20-21 so important? What do these passages tell you about the Word? Let group members share their summaries (p. 13).
- How do John 17:14-17; Hebrews 4:12; and 1 Thessalonians 2:13 explain the importance of God's Word (p. 14)? How do these truths show members how precious they are to God? Let members share how that impacts their hearts.
- What did they learn about Jesus from Hebrew 1:1–2:3? Allow time to share insights from their list or directly from their marked text. How did these truths in Hebrews relate to what they learned in John 17:17? (pp.14-15)
- How do you prepare for difficult days? What did you learn about faith in Hebrews 10:32-39 and Hebrews 11:6? (pp. 18,20)
- According to Hebrews 3:6,14 what does living by faith look like (p. 24)?
- What was Habakkuk's response to hearing that things would get worse (Hab. 3:16-19, p. 23)? Is that living by faith? Could things get worse for you and other believers? How do you need to live?
- In Hebrews 5:11–6:2; 1 Peter 2:1-2; and 1 Corinthians 3:1-4, what does God require to be a spiritually mature believer? (pp. 25-27)
- Look back at 1 Thessalonians 2:13 (p. 14). How does what you learned there relate to maturity? What do you need to do? What are you to long for?
2. Ask how participants can use what they have learned this week to worship God. Give them time to share whatever God has taught them.
3. Encourage them to keep a notebook for listing all the things they learn about God. This is solid food and doing this will help them mature in the faith and "make it" when difficult times come.

Large Group
1. Direct women to turn to the viewer guide for session 2 (p. 32). Make sure women have pens or pencils. Show the second video session.
2. Discuss the group discussion questions from the viewer guide.
3. Ask if any of the women have questions about the video. Invite them to recall and comment on what connected with them.
4. End with prayer asking God to bless each of the women in the coming week.

SESSION 3

Before the Session
1. Pray for each of your group members.
2. Preview the video and answer the questions for week 2.
3. Provide name tags, pencils, and books as needed.

During the Session (Small Group)
Emphasis: Be diligent, not sluggish, Jesus, and the rest of faith.

1. For this week's discussion you may find it flows best to save what was learned in day 1 until later in the discussion.
2. To review the week's study choose from the following questions.
- If time permits, begin with a brief review of week 1. Ask about the value of God's Word. Give a few minutes for sharing what they remember.
- In Hebrews 2:6-11,14-15, (pp. 37-39) what did you learn about Jesus? about the sons of God? From the list they made, discuss Jesus' death and its result.
- What did Hebrews 10:1-5,9-10,12,14-23 tell you about Jesus (pp. 41-43)? Ask about the results of His death in these passages. How were they set free from sin and death? Compare Jesus' sacrifice to the blood of bulls and goats.
- What do Romans 3:9; 5:12; and 6:23 (p. 40) tell you about sin? What did Jesus' death do in relation to sin? (It took care of their sins for all time and cleanses from an evil conscience. Any reminder of sin forgiven by Jesus' death is from the Devil. He loves to discourage the sons of God.)
- According to Hebrews 2:16-18, (p. 44) what should you do when you are tempted to sin? Why? How does verse 18 answer these questions?
- What is "the rest of faith" (pp. 44-48)? How do you enter the rest of faith? The Word united with faith leads to the rest of faith (Heb. 3:7-11; 3:17–4:3).
- What is faith from Hebrews 11:1-2? How would this look in a believer's life?
- What are the exhortations in Hebrews 11:39–12:3 (pp. 51-52)? What did you learn about Jesus in 12:2? How does this relate to Hebrews 2:10?
- Have the group compare Hebrews 11:3 and 1:2-3,10 (the latter passage is from week 1, p. 15). Is it necessary for you to believe this?
- What do you learn from the "hall of faith" that can help you live by faith and have the rest of faith? What did you learn from their examples?
- How does 2 Timothy 2:15 relate to sluggishness? What is the exhortation? Would it solve the problem? How do these things relate to the rest of faith?
3. What have you learned in these two weeks about Jesus that has encouraged you, changed your thinking, or spoken to your heart?

Large Group
1. Direct members to turn to session 3 viewer guide (p. 54). Show the third video session.
2. Discuss the group discussion questions from the viewer guide.
3. Ask if any of the women have questions about the video. Invite them to recall and comment on what connected with them.
4. End with prayer asking God to bless each of the women in the coming week.

SESSION 4

Before the Session

1. Pray for each of your group members.
2. Preview the video and answer the questions in the book for week 3.
3. Small-group leaders, make a list of questions for discussion in your group. Be sure to include those designated for group discussion. Suggested questions appear below in "During the Session."
4. Provide name tags, pencils, and books as needed.

During the Session (Small Group)

1. Welcome women as they arrive.
2. As members arrive, ask them to work in pairs to compile a list of reasons we need a good foundational understanding of the riches God offers us as believers (p. 56).
3. When everyone has arrived and had opportunity to participate, call the group together and pray. Ask for reports from the teams of two.
4. Ask for questions from the week's work. You may wish to discuss:
   - In what ways have you allowed the unfaithfulness of other people to affect the way you perceive the faithfulness of God (p. 59)?
   - Why do you think delaying may decrease our chances of actually doing anything (p. 63)?
   - In what way was Paul's address to the body of Christ at Ephesus ahead of its time in regard to social and racial desegregation (p. 64)?
   - What does it mean to be a member of this new society called the body of Christ (p. 65)?
   - How has God used the most difficult times in your past to draw you into a closer relationship with Him (p. 68)?
   - How do we miss out on the blessings of God's abundant provision when we simply endure seasons rather than seek Him in the midst of our hardships (p. 69)?
   - What relationship do you see between our personal stability despite our current season of life and the object our eyes are fixed upon (p. 73)?

Large Group

1. Direct women to turn to the viewer guide for session 4 (p. 80). Make sure women have pens or pencils. Show the fourth video session.
2. Discuss the group discussion questions from the viewer guide.
3. Ask if any of the women have questions about the video. Invite them to recall and comment on what connected with them.
4. End with prayer.

SESSION 5

Before the Session

1. Pray for each group member.
2. Preview the video and answer the questions in the book for week 4.
3. Small-group leaders, make a list of questions for discussion in your group. Be sure to include those designated for group discussion. Suggested questions appear below in "During the Session."
4. Provide name tags, pencils, and books as needed.

During the Session (Small Group)

1. Welcome women as they arrive.
2. As members arrive, ask them to work together in pairs to compile a list of reasons we forget so quickly how able our God is (p. 82).
3. When everyone has arrived and had opportunity to participate, call the group together and pray. Ask for reports from the teams of two.
4. Ask for questions from the week's work. You may wish to discuss:
   - In what ways do you think you live out the fact that you are indwelled with the turbo power of the Holy Spirit, and in what ways have you lived as though the only strength available to you was your own (p. 84)?
   - How do you think it's possible to know all the right things and all the right answers yet still "not really believe all that stuff" is for you (p. 85)?
   - Why do you think we often become so frustrated with the Lord when we perceive that the answers to our prayers are being delayed (p. 88)?
   - How would you explain to a new believer the idea that God doesn't always cater to our wants (p. 89)?
   - How do you maintain the balance of a truly robust faith with the fact that God has not relinquished His sovereignty to you or anybody else (p. 90)?
   - How would your prayer life change if you fully embraced the truth that God can cover whatever need life throws at you (p. 93)?
   - If someone were to evaluate your prayer life, would she find you to be one who always plays it safe or one who prays expectantly for things beyond her control? What evidence would she see (p. 93)?
   - In what way does sharing our small things with God in prayer help nurture a more intimate relationship with Him (p. 97)?

Large Group

1. Direct women to turn to the viewer guide for session 5 (p. 100). Make sure women have pens or pencils. Show the fifth video session.
2. Discuss the group discussion questions from the viewer guide.
3. Ask if any of the women have questions about the video. Invite them to recall and comment on what connected with them.
4. End with prayer asking God to bless each of the women.

SESSION 6

Before the Session

1. Pray for each group member.
2. Preview the video and answer the questions in the book for week 5.
3. Small-group leaders, make a list of questions for discussion in your group. Be sure to include those designated for group discussion. Suggested questions appear below in "During the Session."
4. Provide name tags, pencils, and books as needed.

During the Session (Small Group)

1. Welcome women as they arrive.
2. As members arrive, ask them to work together in pairs to list the benefits Psalm 37:30-33 describes coming from prompt obedience (p. 104).
3. When everyone has arrived and had opportunity to participate, call the group together and pray. Ask for reports from the teams of two.
4. Ask for questions from the week's work. You may wish to discuss:
   - How would you explain to a new believer the relationship between "knowing" and "obedience" (p. 102)?
   - What part does not just believing in or knowing about Christ but also loving Him make in knowing what to do to obey Him (p. 103)?
   - Why do you think Jesus told His disciples that it was to their advantage that He go away (p. 105)?
   - Why do you think Satan would love to confuse believers about the indwelling of the Holy Spirit (p. 107)?
   - In your own words, define spiritual discernment (p. 108).
   - How does Hebrews 5:11-14 describe the difference between those trained and untrained in spiritual discernment (p. 110)?
   - How does it feel to be "punked" by the Devil (p. 111)?
   - How can you use Psalm 71 to remind yourself not to run away from God when you feel betrayed by someone or a situation (p. 113)?
   - How do you see people in society posing as someone they are not in attempts to feel significant (p. 116)?
   - How does Ephesians 4:25 speak to you about the importance of truth during this "age of the poser" (p. 117)?

Large Group

1. Direct women to turn to the viewer guide for session 6 (p. 122). Make sure everyone has a pen or pencil. Show the sixth video session.
2. Discuss the group discussion questions from the viewer guide.
3. Ask if any of the women have questions about the video. Invite them to recall and comment on what connected with them.
4. End with prayer asking God to bless each of the women in the coming week.

SESSION 7

Before the Session

1. Pray for each group member. After you process the work from week 6, plan to enjoy the panel discussion and celebrate with your group a job well done.
2. Preview the video and answer the questions in the book for week 6.
3. Small-group leaders, make a list of questions for discussion in your group. Be sure to include those designated for group discussion. Suggested questions appear below in "During the Session."
4. Provide name tags, pencils, and books as needed.

During the Session (Small Group)

1. Welcome women as they arrive.
2. As members arrive, ask them to work together in twos or threes to talk about the most valuable things they have gained from this time together.
3. When everyone has arrived and had opportunity to participate, call the group together and pray. Ask for testimonies from those who wish to share.
4. Ask for questions from the week's work. You may wish to discuss:
   - What guidelines do you use to discern if you are sensing something from the Lord or if it's coming from yourself (p. 124)?
   - How have you learned to discern the difference between the leading of the Holy Spirit and the criticism coming from your own nature (p. 125)?
   - Why do you think we need to know whether jealousy is playing a role in a decision we are making (p. 128)?
   - In your own words, describe the difference between being jealous of someone and being jealous for someone (p. 130).
   - What role can pride play in wanting to say or do something out of selfish gain (p. 131)?
   - Why do you think women often struggle so hard with the desire to get in each other's lanes (p. 132)?
   - What are some situations that are prime targets for us to allow our emotions to cloud our discernment (p. 134)?
   - What promise does Proverbs 3:5-7 give to us regarding wisdom and discernment (p. 136)?
   - Why do you think God requires of us this side of the cross to walk in the Spirit rather than simply following a set of rules (p. 138)?
   - When you or I dwell on our sins and beat ourselves up over our failures, are we walking in the Spirit or living by laws? Why (p. 138)?

Large Group

1. Show the panel discussion video.
2. Ask if any of the women have questions about the video. Invite them to recall and comment on what connected with them.
3. End with prayer asking God to bless each of the women as they take the truths they've studied and continue to be faithful, abundant, and true.

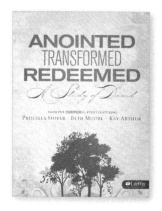
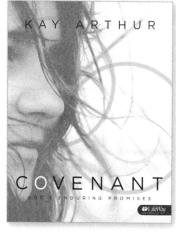

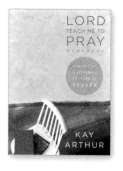

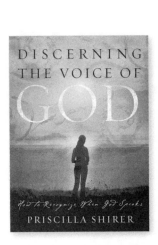

COMPLETE YOUR
BETH MOORE LIBRARY

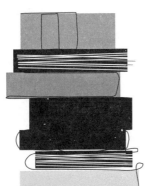

Beth Moore's collection of LifeWay Women Bible studies covers relevant topics from seeking God's heart to loving difficult people. Each in-depth study helps guide you on your journey to find the answers to life's toughest questions. How many have you done?

Go to **lifeway.com/bethmoore** to see the full list and complete your Beth Moore Bible study library.

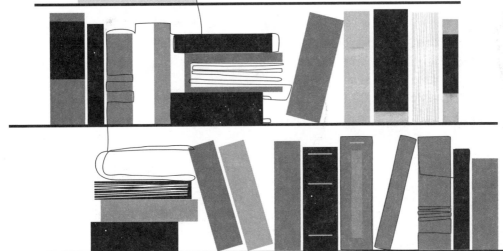

Two Ways to Earn Credit
for Studying LifeWay Christian Resources Material

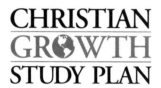

CHRISTIAN GROWTH STUDY PLAN

CONTACT INFORMATION:
Christian Growth Study Plan
One LifeWay Plaza, MSN 117
Nashville, TN 37234
CGSP info line 1-800-968-5519
www.lifeway.com/CGSP
To order resources 1-800-458-2772

Christian Growth Study Plan resources are available for course credit for personal growth and church leadership training.

Courses are designed as plans for personal spiritual growth and for training current and future church leaders. To receive credit, complete the book, material, or activity. Respond to the learning activities or attend group sessions, when applicable, and show your work to your pastor, staff member, or church leader. Then go to *www.lifeway.com/CGSP*, or call the toll-free number for instructions for receiving credit and your certificate of completion.

For information about studies in the Christian Growth Study Plan, refer to the current catalog online at the CGSP Web address. This program and certificate are free LifeWay services to you.

Need a CEU?

CONTACT INFORMATION:
CEU Coordinator
One LifeWay Plaza, MSN 150
Nashville, TN 37234
Info line 1-800-968-5519
www.lifeway.com/CEU

Receive Continuing Education Units (CEUs) when you complete group Bible studies by your favorite LifeWay authors.

Some studies are approved by the Association of Christian Schools International (ACSI) for CEU credits. Do you need to renew your Christian school teaching certificate? Gather a group of teachers or neighbors and complete one of the approved studies. Then go to *www.lifeway.com/CEU* to submit a request form or to find a list of ACSI-approved LifeWay studies and conferences. Book studies must be completed in a group setting. Online courses approved for ACSI credit are also noted on the course list. The administrative cost of each CEU certificate is only $10 per course.

LifeWay
Biblical Solutions for Life